UTAH
COOK BOOK

Compiled by

Bruce & Bobbi Fischer

Cooking Across America
Cookbook Collection™

GOLDEN WEST ☼
PUBLISHERS

Front cover photo by Russ Finley/Finley-Holiday Films
Back Cover photo courtesy National Cattlemen's Beef Association

Acknowledgements

We wish to thank all those who have contributed to this collection of recipes which reflect the tastes and flavors of Utah, including:

Nancy Saxton, Innkeeper, Saltair Bed & Breakfast, Salt Lake City; Chef Tod Gardiner, Iron Blossom Lodge, Wildflower Restaurant, Snowbird; Chef David Jones, Log Haven Restaurant, Salt Lake City; Seven Wives Inn, St. George, Utah CattleWomen and Utah Beef Council: Sharon Kunzler, Chris Freymuller, Connie Tanner, Ruth Ann George, and Scott Parkinson, Winners, Utah Beef Producers Cook-off, Salt Lake City; Joyce Parrish, Salt Lake Area Chamber of Commerce; Jim and Karyn Clark, St. George, Pricilla Lunn and the many other folks of Utah who helped make this an extraordinary collection of recipes reflecting the culinary tastes and delectables of their state.

Other books by Bruce and Bobbi Fischer:

> **_Grand Canyon Cook Book_**
> **_Tortilla Lovers Cook Book_**
> **_Western Breakfast and Brunch Recipes_**
> **_Utah is for Kids! (Activity book)_**

Special thanks to the Junior League of Salt Lake City, Inc. for sharing recipes from their books, *A Pinch of Salt Lake, Always in Season* and *Heritage Cookbook.* Contact them by phone: (801) 328-1019; at their website: www.jlslc.org,; or write: 438 East 200 South, Suite 200, Salt Lake City, UT 84111

ISBN # 1-885590-37-7

Printed in the United States of America

2nd Printing © 2003

Golden West Publishers, Inc.
4113 N. Longview Ave.
Phoenix, AZ 85014, USA
(800) 658-5830

Utah Cook Book

Table of Contents

Utah Cook Book Table of Contents (continued)

Side Dishes

Breads & Muffins

Utah Cook Book Table of Contents (continued)

Tips for High Altitude Cooking

A simple rule of thumb for cooking at higher altitudes: The higher you are, the longer you need to cook most foods. That's because water has a lower boiling point—approximately nine degrees lower for every 5,000-foot gain in elevation. For example, water boils at 212°F at sea level, but at 203° at 5,000 feet. For vegetables, plan to add a bit more liquid and about 7 to 10 percent more cooking time for every 1,000 feet above sea level. Soups will also need to simmer longer; add more liquid as necessary. Meats need no adjustments for altitudes under 7,000 feet, but cook longer and test for doneness at higher elevations.

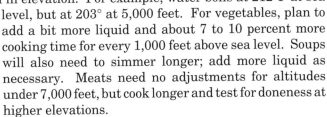

For baking, increase all temperatures by 25°. At 3,000 to 5,000 feet; increase liquids by about 2 tablespoons per cup and decrease baking powder by 1/8 teaspoon for every teaspoon called for in your recipe. At higher altitudes; increase liquids by 3 tablespoons per cup and decrease baking powder by 1/4 teaspoon for every teaspoon. Also, decrease sugar by 2 tablespoons per cup called for in the ingredient list. For altitudes over 7,000, add an extra egg when eggs are included in ingredient list.

Introduction

Utah abounds in breathtaking beauty, colorful history and a diverse cultural background. Its vast deserts, broad valleys and magestic mountain ranges are as awe-inspiring today as they must have been for the people who roamed the land centuries ago.

From the Archaic people to the Anasazi (Pueblo people), and from the Fremont to the Ute, Paiute and Navajo, Native Americans have lived in Utah for more than 10,000 years.

Explorers, trappers and traders followed. John C. Fremont mapped Utah trails and described the land, plants and animals for the U.S. government in the 1840's. The Bartleson-Bidwell pioneer party crossed Utah in 1841 and the Donner party in 1846. Then, the first Mormons entered the Salt Lake Valley on July 24, 1847. Settling the land, they planted, irrigated and tilled the soil.

The Mormons came from the Midwest, led by Brigham Young and other church leaders in search of religious freedom. Their faith and communal focus gave them the strong foundation necessary for community cooperation.

Mormons shared natural resources such as water and timber as they built Salt Lake City and surrounding communities. The church organization served as the first government for the people.

Utah continues to grow and expand. Its cultural institutions such as the Mormon Tabernacle Choir, Ballet West and Utah Symphony are known internationally as well as nationally. Utah has contributed to our world through its educational and research facilities and tourism is at the heart of the economy. Salt Lake City was the host for the 2002 Olympic Winter Games.

Monumental and magnificent national parks, Lake Powell and some of the best skiing in the country make Utah a "must see and do" for tourists and natives alike.

Enjoy these tastes of Utah!

Utah Facts & Information

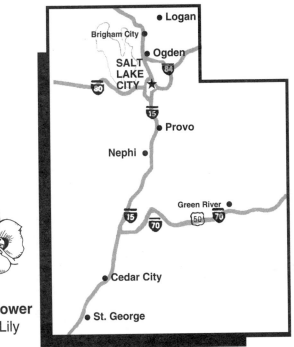

State Flower
Sego Lily

State Population — 2,233,169 (2000)
Statehood — Jan. 4, 1896 - 45th state
State Capital — Salt Lake City
State Nickname —The Beehive State
State Motto — *Industry*
State Area — 84,904 sq. mi.
Highest Elevation — Kings Peak, 13,528
State Symbol — Beehive
State Fossil— Allosaurus
State Animal — Rocky Mountain Elk
State Fish — Bonneville Cutthroat Trout
State Gem — Topaz
State Cooking Pot — Dutch Oven
State Rock — Coal
State Insect — Honeybee
State Fruit — Cherry
For more information about Utah: http://www.ce.ex.state.ut.

State Bird
California Gull

State Tree
Blue Spruce

A Sampling of Utah Food Festivals

Chocolate Festival — Logan — February
Black & White Days (Dairy) — Richmond — May
Living Traditions Festival — Salt Lake City — May
Scandinavian Days — Ephraim — May
Strawberry Days — Pleasant Grove — June
Festival of the American West (Dutch Oven) —
    Wellsville — July
Cherry Days — North Ogden — July
Turkey Days — Moroni — July
Duck Creek Days Chili Cook-Off — Duck Creek — July
Greek Festival — Price — July
Lamb Days — Fountain Green
    City — July
Raspberry Days — Garden
    City — August
Apple Days — River Heights — August
Corn Festival — Enterprise — August
Wheat & Beet Days – Garland – August
Trout & Berry Days — Paradise — August
Salmon Supper — Payson — August
Slovenian Days — Price — August
Swiss Days — Midway — August/September
Peach Days – Brigham City – September
Sauerkraut Festival — Providence — September
Golden Onion Days — Payson — September
Octoberfest — Snowbird — Sept.-Oct.
Melon Days — Green River — September
Tomato Days — Hooper — September
Peach Days — Ferron City — September
Utah State Fair — Salt Lake City — September

For more information about the events listed above, contact
local Chambers of Commerce.

Appetizers & Beverages

Kalitsounia
(Greek Cheese Patties)

"These patties are always served during our Greek Festival which we celebrate each year on the 2nd weekend in July."

Athena Kontas—Price

2 lbs. fresh RICOTTA
1 pkg. (8 oz.) CREAM CHEESE
3 EGGS
1 tsp. SUGAR
1/4 cup chopped fresh MINT
   or 2 Tbsp. dry, crushed
1/2 tsp. SALT
Dash of CINNAMON

Mix all ingredients together until creamy, cover and refrigerate. Use flour and water to make a stiff dough (adding 2 tablespoons of oil if desired). Knead until smooth; cover and let stand about an hour before rolling out. Roll dough to one-eighth-inch thickness and cut into four-and-one-half-inch rounds. Place 1 tablespoon of cheese mixture in center of each round, moisten edges and fold rounds in half. Press edges with tines of a fork to seal. Deep fry in hot vegetable oil or bake on greased pan in a 400° oven for about 20 minutes.

Glen Canyon Dip

3 ripe AVOCADOS
2 tsp. LEMON JUICE
1 cup SOUR CREAM
1 cup MAYONNAISE
1 pkg. TACO SEASONING
2 cans (9 oz. ea.) BEAN DIP

1 bunch GREEN ONIONS, chopped
3 med. TOMATOES, chopped
1 can (6 oz.) pitted OLIVES, sliced
8 oz. CHEDDAR CHEESE, grated

Peel and mash avocados in a bowl, add lemon juice and set aside. Combine sour cream, mayonnaise and taco seasoning in another bowl and set aside. Spread bean dip on a serving plate, spread avocado mixture over bean dip and then layer with sour cream mixture. Top with onions, tomatoes and olives and sprinkle all with cheese. Serve with your favorite chips or crackers.

Glen Canyon Dam & Recreation Area

The Glen Canyon Dam, built on the Colorado River in Arizona was completed in 1964. The dam created Lake Powell which is 186 miles long and has 2,000 miles of shoreline. The Glen Canyon Recreation Area, shared by both Arizona and Utah, offers a multitude of outdoor opportunities.

Shrimp Stuffed Artichokes

2-4 ARTICHOKES
1 pkg. (16 oz.) frozen SHRIMP
1 cup chopped CELERY

2 Tbsp. LEMON JUICE
1/2 cup MAYONNAISE
SALT and PEPPER to taste

Boil artichokes, cool and chill. Defrost shrimp, mix with remaining ingredients and chill. When ready to serve, gently push artichoke leaves outward, fill with shrimp mixture and serve with dressing of choice.

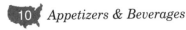

Five Fingers Cheese Strips

1/2 cup BUTTER or MARGARINE
1 cup WATER
1 cup FLOUR
1 tsp. CHILI POWDER
1 tsp. ground CUMIN
1 tsp. dried CORIANDER, crushed
1/2 tsp. DRY MUSTARD
4 EGGS
1 cup diced, cooked HAM
1/2 cup grated MONTEREY JACK CHEESE and JALAPEÑO
    PEPPER CHEESE, combined

Melt butter in a saucepan. Add water and bring to a boil. Stir together flour, chili powder, cumin, coriander, and mustard. Add flour mixture to butter mixture; stir vigorously. Cook and stir until mixture forms a firm ball. Remove from heat; cool slightly, about 5 minutes. Add eggs, one at a time, beating with a wooden spoon for 1 to 2 minutes after each addition or until smooth. Stir in ham and cheese. Spoon dough into a pastry tube fitted with a 1/2-inch tip opening*. Slowly pipe dough onto a greased baking sheet into strips about 3 inches long, keeping them one inch apart. Bake in a 375° oven for 15 to 20 minutes or until golden and puffy. Serve warm.

*Dough may also be dropped from a teaspoon onto a greased cookie sheet and pressed lightly with a spoon to form disks.

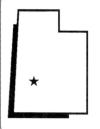

Fremont Indian State Park

At Fremont Indian State Park, off Highway 89 near Richfield, the museum displays artifacts and pictographs from nearby Five Fingers Hill. About 10 miles southeast lie the multicolored rock formations of Big Rock Candy Mountain.

Mexican Hat Salsa

1 tsp. DRY OREGANO
15 sprigs fresh CILANTRO*
1/3 tsp. CUMIN, ground
1-2 cloves GARLIC, minced
1-2 dry TEPIN CHILES, chopped

1 can (8 oz.) TOMATO SAUCE
SALT to taste
1 tsp. (scant) VINEGAR
1/2 cup WATER

Blend together oregano, cilantro, cumin, garlic, and tepin chile. Add remaining ingredients, and blend again. Chill several hours or overnight. Serve with anything!

*Dry cilantro may be substituted.

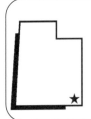

Mexican Hat

The city of Mexican Hat is at the entrance to the Navajo Indian Reservation and Monument Valley. It is named after a nearby rock formation resembling a Mexican sombrero that balances on a 200-foot cliff.

Marinated Mushrooms

12-24 large fresh MUSHROOMS
1 BERMUDA ONION, finely diced

Italian-style SALAD
DRESSING

In a bowl, combine onions and dressing and add mushrooms. Stir well. Add a small plate to hold mushrooms down and refrigerate for two to four hours before serving.

Chile & Ham Roll-ups

1 can (4 oz.) diced GREEN CHILES
1 pkg. (3 oz.) CREAM CHEESE
10-12 slices HAM LUNCH MEAT

Combine chiles and cream cheese and spread on ham slices. Roll up tightly. Cut in halves or quarters and skewer with toothpicks. Chill before serving.

Seafood Mousse

"This is a super hor d'oeuvre recipe that everyone enjoys."

Jim and Karyn Clark—St. George

1 env. (1 oz.) unflavored GELATIN
1/4 cup cold WATER
1 can (10.75 oz.) undiluted CREAM of MUSHROOM SOUP
1 pkg. (8 oz.) CREAM CHEESE, softened
1 cup MAYONNAISE
3/4 cup finely chopped CELERY
1 1/2-2 cups SHRIMP or CRABMEAT
1/2 cup chopped GREEN ONIONS
1 1/4 tsp. WORCESTERSHIRE SAUCE

In a small bowl, soften gelatin in cold water. In a medium saucepan, heat soup and add gelatin, stirring well. Add cream cheese, beating until smooth. Add remaining ingredients and pour into a 4-cup mold. Refrigerate overnight. Unmold onto a platter and serve as a salad or as an appetizer with crackers.

Did You Know?

Salt Lake City was founded on July 24, 1847 by a group of Mormon pioneers (148 people in all) led by Brigham Young.

Chili-Grape Meatballs

1 lb. GROUND BEEF
1/2 cup BREAD CRUMBS
1/3 cup minced ONIONS
1/4 cup MILK
1 EGG
1 Tbsp. PARSLEY
1 tsp. SALT
1/8 tsp. PEPPER
1/2 tsp. WORCESTERSHIRE
 SAUCE
2/3 cup CHILI SAUCE
1 1/4 cups GRAPE JELLY

Mix together all ingredients except chili sauce and grape jelly. Form into meatballs and brown in a skillet. In a saucepan, heat chili sauce and grape jelly until melted. Add meatballs and simmer for 30 minutes. Skewer meatballs with toothpicks and serve with sauce on the side.

Zion Yogurt-Dill Dip

1 cup SOUR CREAM
1 cup MAYONNAISE
1 Tbsp. ground PARSLEY
2 tsp. minced ONIONS
2 tsp. DILL WEED
1/2 cup PLAIN YOGURT

Mix all ingredients well. Refrigerate overnight. Try with your favorite raw vegetables, crackers, chips or baked potatoes.

Zion National Park

From Zion Canyon, a spectacular gorge that lies just inside the southern entrance of Zion National Park, to Kolob Canyon, and Kolob Arch in the northwest corner of the Park, you will find a visit here an unparalleled adventure.

Cheese & Chile Bites

1 1/2 lbs. MONTEREY JACK CHEESE, grated
3/4 lb. CHEDDAR CHEESE, grated
1/4 cup diced GREEN CHILES
3 EGGS, beaten
1 Tbsp. FLOUR
1/4 cup MILK

Combine cheeses. Spread half of the cheese mixture in a greased 9 x 13 baking pan. Spread chiles over top of cheese. Top with remaining cheese. Combine eggs, flour and milk and mix well. Pour evenly over cheese mixture. Bake at 375° for 45 minutes or until light brown. Let stand 5 minutes before cutting into small squares.

Cedar Breaks Berry Cooler

6 oz. frozen LIMEADE concentrate
1 bottle (16 oz.) CRANBERRY JUICE COCKTAIL
1/4 cup ORANGE-FLAVORED INSTANT BREAKFAST DRINK
ICE CUBES
FRESH MINT

Prepare limeade according to package directions. Stir in cranberry juice cocktail and instant breakfast drink until dissolved. Pour limeade mixture over ice in tall glasses. Garnish each with a fresh sprig of mint.

Cedar Breaks National Monument

The entrance to this monument is south-east of Cedar City on SR 14. Here, a 3-mile-wide amphitheater that is nearly 2,500 feet in depth was caused by erosion of the natural limestone cliffs. Early settlers thought the juniper trees that rim the base of the monument were cedar trees. Hence its name.

Hot & Spicy Cider

3 ORANGES
3 (6") CINNAMON STICKS
3 tsp. WHOLE ALLSPICE
48 WHOLE CLOVES

1 gal. APPLE CIDER
2 qts. CRANBERRY JUICE
3/4 cup SUGAR
3 tsp. BUTTER

Squeeze juice from oranges. Cut orange peels into chunks and place in a cheesecloth bag along with cinnamon sticks, allspice and cloves. Place cheesecloth bag in a large saucepan* and add juices, sugar and butter. Heat to almost boiling, remove from heat and serve.

*Or, place bag in the basket of a 30-cup percolator. Add juices, sugar and butter to the percolator and allow to perk for 10 minutes.

Perfect Wedding Party Punch

"This recipe was submitted to Rainbow Gardens by Ms. Jean Shaum. We use it as part of our refreshments offered during our famous annual April Bridal Shower event."

Robert Peery King—Rainbow Gardens, Ogden

1 can (46 oz.) PINEAPPLE JUICE, chilled
1/2 gal. VANILLA ICE CREAM, softened
1/2 gal. LIME SHERBET, softened
2-3 bottles GINGER ALE, chilled
1 Tbsp. NUTMEG

Pour pineapple juice into punch bowl. Add ice cream, sherbet and ginger ale. Stir and then sprinkle with nutmeg.

Did You Know?

The Four Corners Monument marks the only place in the United States where four states meet: Utah, Arizona, Colorado and New Mexico.

Saltair Fruit Smoothie

Nancy serves this most refreshing smoothie to her guests. She is pleased to share her secret with you.

Nancy Saxton—Saltair Bed & Breakfast, Salt Lake City

1-2 BANANAS (depending on thickness of smoothie you prefer)
10-12 ICE CUBES
1 1/2 cups VANILLA YOGURT
6 oz. MIXED FRUIT CONCENTRATE

Place all ingredients in a blender. Add water to fill blender and blend until smooth.

Serves 4-6.

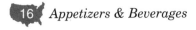

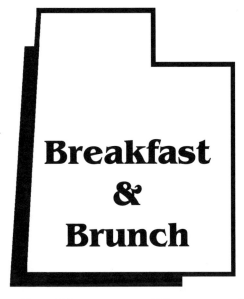

Apple-Pecan Pancakes

"This was my mother's favorite recipe."

Donna Curtis—Seven Wives Inn, St. George

3 APPLES, peeled, cored
   and diced
1/2 cup WHITE SUGAR
2 tsp. CINNAMON
1/4 cup WATER
4 cups FLOUR
5 tsp. BAKING POWDER
1 tsp. SALT

1 tsp. CINNAMON
1 tsp. NUTMEG
4 EGGS, beaten
2/3 cup BROWN SUGAR
2 tsp. VANILLA
4 cups HALF & HALF
1/2 cup BUTTER, melted
   and cooled

Place apples in a microwave safe bowl with white sugar, cinnamon and water. Mix well and microwave on High for 4-5 minutes. Set aside. In a large bowl, combine flour, baking powder, salt, cinnamon and nutmeg. In a separate bowl combine eggs, brown sugar, vanilla and half & half. Add melted butter and mix well. Add the liquid ingredients to the dry ingredients and mix well. Fold in apple mixture and mix well. Spoon dough onto a hot griddle and cook until done.

Serves 10-12.

Utah Strawberry Days Waffles

"A sourdough variety for people who love crisp, light waffles."

Heritage Cookbook (Sandy Snow Ellsworth)
Junior League of Salt Lake City, Inc., Salt Lake City

3/4 cup SOURDOUGH STARTER, see page 75
2 cups FLOUR
1 1/2 cups WARM WATER
2 Tbsp. SUGAR
1/4 tsp. BAKING SODA
3/4 tsp. SALT
2 EGG WHITES
2 EGG YOLKS, beaten
1/4 cup VEGETABLE OIL
1 cup HEAVY CREAM
2 Tbsp. SUGAR
2 cups fresh STRAWBERRIES, sliced

Put sourdough starter in a large bowl. Gradually mix in flour. Thoroughly blend in warm water. Cover. Put in warm place overnight (90°). Next day, combine sugar, baking soda and salt. Set aside. Beat egg whites just until stiff peaks form. Set aside. Mix egg yolks and vegetable oil into sourdough starter. Stir in sugar mixture. Gently fold in egg whites. Pour into hot waffle iron and bake 4 to 5 minutes (until golden brown). While baking waffles, whip heavy cream and 2 tablespoons sugar together. To serve, put a scoop of whipped cream on each waffle. Top with fresh strawberries.

Yield: 4 waffles.

Did You Know?

Utah was named for the resident American Indian tribe, the Utes. In the Ute language, "Yuta" means "home on mountain top."

Oat Crunch Breakfast

This is a high-energy boost combination. Serve as a breakfast cereal or use as a great trail mix!

5 cups OATS	1 cup WHEAT GERM
3/4 cup LIGHT OIL	1/2 cup WATER
1 cup slivered ALMONDS	1/2 Tbsp. SALT
3/4 cup HONEY	1 Tbsp. VANILLA
1 cup COCONUT	SUNFLOWER SEEDS

Mix all ingredients together and spread on a baking sheet. Toast in oven for 1/2 hour at 300°. Stir every 10 minutes.

Did You Know?
Precipitation in Utah varies from an average of less than five inches in the Great Salt Lake Desert to more than 60 inches in the Wasatch Mountains. The average annual precipitation is between 10-15 inches per year.

Chiles Rellenos Casserole

Jim Clark—St. George

12 EGGS, beaten
1 pint SOUR CREAM
1 1/2 tsp. SALT
3-4 cans (7 oz. ea.) GREEN CHILE STRIPS
1/2 lb. SHARP CHEDDAR CHEESE, sliced or grated
1/2 lb. MILD CHEDDAR CHEESE, sliced or grated

Preheat oven to 350°. Grease the bottom of a 9 x 13 pan. In a bowl, combine eggs and sour cream and mix well. Add salt and mix. Set aside. Cover bottom of greased pan with chile strips and layer with cheeses. Continue layering until all of the chiles and cheeses are used up. Pour egg mixture over all and bake in 350° oven for 50 minutes. Let cool 10 minutes before serving.

Mountain Man Breakfast

"This is one of our favorite camping and church breakfasts."

Lamar Cox—Payson

1 lb. SPICY PORK SAUSAGE
1 lg. ONION, finely chopped
2 lbs. HASH BROWNS
12 EGGS

Chopped GREEN BELL PEPPERS
1 lb. SHARP CHEDDAR CHEESE
SALT and PEPPER to taste

In a skillet*, brown sausage and then sauté onions. Remove sausage and pour off most of the drippings. Add hash browns and cook until brown. Return sausage and onions to skillet and add eggs. Add bell peppers and season to taste. Stir well and then sprinkle cheese over top. Bake in a preheated oven at 350° for 15 to 20 minutes.

*Over a campfire, use a Dutch oven to prepare this breakfast. When ready to bake, place hot coals on lid of oven.

Brittlebush Brunch

1/4 cup BUTTER
1/4 cup FLOUR
1 cup SOUR CREAM
1 cup MILK
1/4 tsp. chopped fresh THYME
1/4 tsp. chopped fresh CHIVES
1/4 tsp. chopped fresh SWEET BASIL
1/4 cup chopped fresh PARSLEY
2 cups shredded CHEDDAR CHEESE
18 hard-boiled EGGS, sliced
1 lb. BACON, cooked and crumbled
1 cup seasoned STUFFING MIX

In a medium saucepan, melt butter and slowly blend in flour. Stir for 2 minutes until cooked and slightly thickened. Add sour cream and milk; blend well. Add fresh herbs and cheese. Cook on low heat until cheese has melted. Arrange sliced eggs and bacon in a 9 x 13 casserole. Pour sauce over top and sprinkle with stuffing mix. Bake at 350° for 25 minutes.

Serves 12.

Golden Chiles Rellenos

4 POBLANO CHILES, roasted, peeled and seeded*

1 lb. GROUND BEEF	**2 EGGS, beaten**
1 ONION, diced	**FLOUR**
2 fresh TOMATOES, diced	**OIL**
SALT and PEPPER to taste	

*Place chiles under a broiler and broil, turning often, so that they become evenly blackened on all sides. Place in a plastic bag for 10-15 minutes, this loosens the skins and makes them easy to slide off. Make a slit up one side of each chile, lengthwise, and remove the seed sack and any loose seeds.

Sauté meat, drain fat and add onion, tomatoes, salt and pepper. Cook until meat is browned. Stuff peppers with meat mixture. Dip stuffed peppers into beaten eggs, then in flour. Fry in oil until golden brown.

Bluff Waffles

3/4 cup MILK	**1/4 tsp. SALT**
1 tsp. VANILLA	**2 Tbsp. CORN OIL**
1 tsp. BAKING POWDER	**3/4 cup FLOUR**
1 EGG, beaten	

Mix the above ingredients together until they make a thin batter. Ladle onto preheated waffle iron and bake until golden brown. Serve warm with syrup, butter and jelly.

Bluff

Bluff is the oldest community in Southeastern Utah. Sandstone homes built as long ago as 1880 may still be seen here. Hiking, bicycling and even llama tours kick off at Bluff as well as raft, kayak and dory trips down the San Juan River to Lake Powell, or down the Colorado River to Cataract Canyon.

Breakfast Bundt Pan Rolls

Karyn Clark—St. George

1/2 cup CHOPPED NUTS
2/3 pkg. (approx. 20) FROZEN WHITE BREAD ROLLS
1 pkg. (3 oz.) INSTANT BUTTERSCOTCH PUDDING
1 stick MARGARINE, melted
1/2 cup BROWN SUGAR
CINNAMON to taste
RAISINS

Grease bundt pan thoroughly. Sprinkle chopped nuts onto bottom of pan. Place approximately 20 rolls in pan, spreading evenly over the nuts. Sprinkle butterscotch pudding over the top. In a separate pan, melt one stick of margarine; add brown sugar and cinnamon. Stir well. Pour butter mixture over rolls and sprinkle with raisins. Place rolls in cold oven overnight or for at least 6-7 hours. Remove rolls and preheat oven to 350°. Bake rolls 20-30 minutes or until browned. Remove pan from oven, turn rolls over and serve warm.

St. George

St. George was settled by the Mormons during the Civil War. They were sent to the area by Brigham Young to raise cotton, which, due to the war, was in short supply. The St. George Mormon Temple, built 1869-1877, was the first Mormon Temple to be built in Utah. The Mormon tabernacle built here in 1863 supports a 140-foot steeple!

Salads, Soups & Stews

Pineapple-Mint Salad

"Many kinds of salads can be found at almost every get-together in Utah, but a gelatin salad is always the favorite."

Aldine Smith—Salt Lake City

1 can (20 oz.) CRUSHED PINEAPPLE
1 env. unflavored GELATIN
2 drops GREEN FOOD COLORING
1/3 cup MINT-FLAVORED APPLE JELLY
1 cup WHIPPING CREAM
1 tsp. POWDERED SUGAR

Drain pineapple, reserving 1/2 cup juice. Blend gelatin, food coloring and pineapple juice; bring to a boil, stirring constantly. Add apple jelly. Stir mixture over medium heat until gelatin has dissolved and jelly has melted. Mix in crushed pineapple and cool. Whip cream with sugar until stiff peaks form. Fold cream mixture into jelly mixture. Refrigerate until firm. Garnish with mint.

Serves 6-8.

Indian Paintbrush Fruit Salad

1 pkg. (5 oz.) instant LEMON PUDDING
6 cups (combined) fresh, sliced FRUITS, such as:
- • PEACHES
- • STRAWBERRIES
- • GRAPES
- • APRICOTS
- • CANTALOUPE
- • MELON

1 can (16 oz.) crushed PINEAPPLE, undrained
1 can (8 oz.) MANDARIN ORANGES, undrained
1/2 bag miniature MARSHMALLOWS
chopped NUTS
1 lg. container COOL WHIP®
2 BANANAS

Pour dry pudding mix into a large bowl. Add the fruit (except bananas), marshmallows, nuts and Cool Whip (reserving a portion of the Cool Whip for garnish). Cover and chill salad overnight. Just before serving, peel and cut bananas into bite-sized pieces and fold into pudding mixture. Top with dollops of reserved Cool Whip.

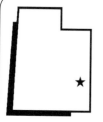

Moab

In pioneer days, Moab was familiar to Butch Cassidy and the Sundance Kid as well as many other outlaw gangs and became a favorite location for Zane Grey's western novels. Moab is known as the "gateway" to Arches and Canyonlands National Parks, Dead Horse Point State Park, the LaSal Mountains and the mighty Colorado River.

Sombrero-Style Cottage Cheese Salad

1/2 cup PINEAPPLE JUICE
2 1/2 cups dry curd COTTAGE CHEESE
SALT and PEPPER to taste
1/2 tsp. CHILI POWDER
6 slices PINEAPPLE
GREEN BELL PEPPER, cut into strips
LETTUCE

Mix pineapple juice, cottage cheese, chili powder, salt and pepper. Arrange lettuce leaves on individual salad plates. Place a slice of pineapple in the center of each. Mold cottage-cheese mixture into cones 2-inches in diameter at base and set one on each pineapple slice. Arrange pepper strips around cottage cheese cones to resemble hat bands. Serve with any desired dressing.

Serves 6.

Macaroni & Bacon Salad

1 pkg. (16 oz.) small SHELL MACARONI
1 bunch GREEN ONIONS, chopped
1 jar (4 oz.) PIMENTOS
1 can (2 oz.) BLACK OLIVES, sliced
1 lb. BACON, cooked, drained, and crumbled
2/3 cup sliced CELERY
6 hard-boiled EGGS, chopped

Dressing:
    1/2 can (10 oz.) TOMATO SOUP
    1/2 cup MAYONNAISE
    1 Tbsp. WORCESTERSHIRE SAUCE
    1/2 Tbsp. HORSERADISH

Prepare macaroni according to package directions. Drain and rinse well. Mix all salad ingredients together. Whisk together all dressing ingredients. Pour dressing over salad and toss well. Chill and serve.

Canyonlands Salad

1 pkg. (16 oz.) MACARONI SHELLS
1/2 cup sliced GREEN ONIONS (with tops)
1/4 cup cooked and crumbled BACON
1 cup MAYONNAISE
1/4 cup LEMON JUICE
3 Tbsp. grated PARMESAN CHEESE
1 tsp. SUGAR
1/2 tsp. GARLIC POWDER
4 cups (bite-sized pieces) SALAD GREENS
1 medium ZUCCHINI, sliced
1 cup sliced CAULIFLOWER
1 cup BROCCOLI FLOWERETS
2 med. TOMATOES, cut into wedges

Cook macaroni according to package directions; drain. Rinse with cold water and drain again. Stir together macaroni, onions and 2 tablespoons of bacon in medium bowl. Mix mayonnaise, lemon juice, cheese, sugar and garlic powder together and stir into macaroni mixture. In a 3 1/2 quart salad bowl, layer salad greens, macaroni mixture, zucchini, cauliflower, broccoli and tomatoes. Pour your favorite dressing evenly over the top. Cover and refrigerate at least 2 hours. Sprinkle with balance of bacon just before serving.

Canyonlands National Park

Canyonlands National Park has elevations that range from 3,720 ft. to 6,987 ft. The confluence of the Green and Colorado Rivers divides the park into 3 districts. The northern district, Island in the Sky, is a huge level mesa featuring Upheaval Dome and Grand View Point. The Needles District has multicolored rock spires that overshadow meadowlands and natural parks. The Maze District on the western edge of the park encompasses the Land of Standing Rocks, the Maze and Horseshoe Canyon.

Peaks Potato Salad

7 med. POTATOES, cooked in jackets, peeled and diced
1/3 cup clear FRENCH or ITALIAN dressing
3/4 cup chopped CELERY
1/3 cup chopped GREEN ONIONS
4 EGGS, hard-cooked, separated
1 cup MAYONNAISE
1/2 cup SOUR CREAM
1 1/2 tsp. prepared HORSERADISH SAUCE
SALT, PEPPER and CELERY SEED to taste
1/3 cup diced CUCUMBER

While potatoes are still warm, pour dressing over top and chill for 2 hours. Remove from refrigerator, add celery, and onion. Chop egg whites and add to potato mixture. Mash yolks. Reserving some of the yolks for garnish, combine yolks with mayonnaise, sour cream and horseradish. Fold into salad. Add salt, pepper and celery seed to taste. Chill mixture for 2 hours. Add cucumber, sprinkle reserved yolk over top and serve.

Hot Turkey Salad

"This is a great way to make use of leftover turkey."

Iantha Folkman—Brigham City Senior Center, Brigham City

2 cups cubed TURKEY
2 Tbsp. grated ONION
2 cups thinly sliced CELERY
2 Tbsp. LEMON JUICE
1 cup MAYONNAISE
SALT and PEPPER to taste
1/2 cup chopped toasted
   ALMONDS
1 cup toasted BREAD CUBES
1/3 cup grated CHEDDAR CHEESE

In a large bowl, combine turkey, onion, celery, lemon juice and mayonnaise. Add salt and pepper to taste and fold in the almonds. Place mixture in a casserole dish, spread bread cubes and cheese over top and bake at 450° for 10 to 15 minutes.

Marinated Carrot Salad

"This a favorite dish at our Senior Center."

Iantha Folkman—Brigham City Senior Center, Brigham City

2 lbs. CARROTS, cut into 1/4" slices (or use baby carrots)
1 BERMUDA ONION, chopped
1 GREEN BELL PEPPER, chopped
1 can (10.75 oz.) TOMATO SOUP
3/4 cup VINEGAR
3/4 cup SUGAR
1/2 cup OIL
1 tsp. DRY MUSTARD
1 tsp. WORCESTERSHIRE SAUCE

Cook carrots until just tender. Drain. Add balance of ingredients. Cover and chill for at least 12 hours (or up to 2 weeks).

Serves 15.

The Enterprise Corn Festival

Held the last Saturday in August, the corn festival features a Dutch Oven Dinner, melodramas performed 3 times a day, street dancing, a rodeo and much more!

Corn Salad

2 cans (15 oz. ea.) CORN
1 can (15 oz.) PETITE PEAS
1 can (14 oz.) GREEN BEANS
1 jar (4 oz.) PIMENTOS, diced
1 ONION , chopped or 1 bunch GREEN ONIONS, diced
1 GREEN BELL PEPPER, chopped
Dressing:

3/4 cup VINEGAR	**1/2 cup OIL**
3/4 cup SUGAR	**SALT and PEPPER to taste**

Combine the first 6 ingredients. Place dressing ingredients in a saucepan, bring to a boil and boil for 10 minutes. Cool. Pour dressing over vegetables. Let stand overnight if possible. Stir several times.

Southwestern Tenderloin Salad

Ruth Ann George's prize winning recipe of the 1997 Utah Beef Producers Cook-Off.

Utah Cattle Women & Utah Beef Council, Salt Lake City

1 1/4 lbs. TENDERLOIN STEAKS
2 cups SALSA
1 cup fat-free RANCH DRESSING
6 cups SALAD GREENS
3/4 cup thinly sliced GREEN ONIONS
1/2 cup shredded CARROTS
2 cups chopped TOMATOES
1 1/2 cups KIDNEY BEANS, rinsed and drained

Marinate tenderloin in 1 cup salsa for 20 minutes. Mix ranch dressing and 1 cup salsa together and refrigerate. Grill or broil steak to desired doneness. Toss salad greens, green onion and carrots together. Layer greens mixture, tomatoes, and kidney beans on a platter or in a shallow salad bowl. Slice tenderloin thinly and arrange on top of salad. Serve ranch dressing and salsa mixture on the side.

Serves 4.

Grandma Madsen's Dumplings

"My great-great-grandmother was a Mormon pioneer who emigrated from Denmark. We love these dumplings in home-made chicken soup. (The nutmeg is the secret!)"

Pat Conover—Editor, Springville Herald, Springville

2 cups MILK   **4 EGGS**
1 stick BUTTER   **NUTMEG to taste**
1 cup FLOUR

Place milk, butter and flour in a saucepan. Cook, stirring constantly, until it forms a ball. Remove from stove. Whip in the eggs and stir in nutmeg to taste. Drop from a teaspoon into hot soup. Allow dumplings to cook slowly until done.

Kitchen Kettle Soup

2 lbs. lean HAMBURGER
1/3 cup dried SPLIT PEAS
SALT and PEPPER to taste
1/4 tsp. OREGANO
1/4 tsp. BASIL
6 cups boiling WATER
1 cup uncooked ELBOW MACARONI
1 pkg. DRY ONION SOUP MIX
1 can (8 oz.) TOMATO SAUCE
1 Tbsp. SOY SAUCE
1 cup thinly sliced CELERY
1/4 cup chopped CELERY LEAVES
1 cup thinly sliced CARROTS
CHEDDAR CHEESE, grated

In a large kettle, brown hamburger and drain. Add the following ingredients: peas, salt, pepper, oregano, basil, water, macaroni, soup mix, tomato sauce, and soy sauce. Cover and simmer for 25 minutes. Add celery, celery leaves and carrots to hamburger mixture. Continue cooking for 15 minutes. Serve, garnished with cheddar cheese.

Salt Lake City

Founded in 1847 by Brigham Young, Salt Lake City is the home of the world headquarters of the Church of Jesus Christ of Latter-Day Saints, (also known as the Mormon Church). Be sure to see Eagle Gate here. This giant arch is surmounted by a 4,000-pound statue of an eagle with a wingspread of 20 feet. The Family History Library has one of the world's largest collections of genealogical information. The Brigham Young Monument and the Mormon Tabernacle are also well-known sites to visit in this fascinating city.

Albondigas Soup

(Meatball Soup)

1 1/2 lbs. lean GROUND BEEF
1/2 cup cooked WHITE RICE
1 can (4 oz.) diced GREEN CHILES
GARLIC to taste
SALT and PEPPER to taste
2 Tbsp. fresh CILANTRO, chopped
Dash of CUMIN
2 EGGS
1 can (28 oz.) WHOLE TOMATOES
3 1/2 cups WATER
1 can (10 oz.) BEEF BROTH
1/2 cup sliced CARROTS
1/2 cup chopped CELERY
1/2 cup diced GREEN BELL PEPPER
1/2 cup diced ONION

In a large bowl, combine beef, rice, green chiles, garlic, salt, pepper, cilantro, cumin, and eggs. Mix well and then shape into 1-inch meatballs. In a large pot, combine tomatoes, water, broth, carrots, celery, bell peppers and onion and stir. Bring to a boil; add meatballs and simmer for 20 minutes.

Pioneer Stew

1 1/2 lbs. STEW MEAT, cut
    into 1" cubes
WATER
1 BAY LEAF
4 ONIONS, chopped
6 CARROTS, diced

4 med. RED POTATOES,
    quartered
2 Tbsp. PAPRIKA
SALT and PEPPER to taste
4 Tbsp. FLOUR
1 cup COLD WATER

Brown stew meat in a heavy skillet. When well browned, cover with water and let simmer until tender. Add bay leaf, onions, carrots and potatoes. Add paprika. Salt and pepper to taste. To thicken; mix the flour in 1 cup of cold water until it is a smooth paste. Add to stew, stirring constantly. Remove bay leaf before serving.

Steak Tortilla Soup

Conny Tanner's prize-winning recipe of the 1997 Utah Beef Producers Cook-Off.

Utah Cattle Women & Utah Beef Council, Salt Lake City

1-1 /2 lbs. TOP SIRLOIN STEAK, cut into 1/4" pieces

Marinade:
   2 Tbsp. WATER
   1 tsp. VEGETABLE OIL
   1 Tbsp. SOY SAUCE
   1 1/2 tsp. SUGAR
   1 tsp. CORNSTARCH

Broth:
   2 cups BEEF STOCK
   1/2 med. ONION, chopped
   3 cloves GARLIC, minced or 1/4 tsp. dried GARLIC, minced
   1 can (28 oz.) diced TOMATOES
   1 can (10 oz.) mild ENCHILADA SAUCE
   1 can (4 oz.) diced GREEN CHILES
   1/8 tsp. CUMIN
   SALT and PEPPER to taste

Garnish:
   20-30 TORTILLA CHIPS
   1 1/2 cups shredded MONTEREY JACK CHEESE
   4-6 AVOCADO SLICES
   2 Tbsp. CILANTRO, chopped

Combine marinade ingredients and add beef. Refrigerate. In a medium saucepan, mix broth ingredients. Bring to a boil (the longer you boil it the "hotter" the flavor). Reduce heat and simmer. Heat a large non-stick skillet over medium-high heat. Add beef and marinade mixture, one half at a time. Stir-fry each half for 1-2 minutes or until outsides are no longer pink. Divide tortilla chips into bowls and ladle broth over top. Spoon beef into each bowl. Sprinkle with cheese and garnish with avocado slices and cilantro.

Serves 4-6.

Summer Stew

Early pioneer cooks provided very simple, yet nourishing recipes for their households. This recipe from the mid-1800s is typical of that fare.

2 lg. POTATOES, cut into small pieces
2 lg. ONIONS, chopped
WATER
1 (3" square) piece of SALT PORK
SALT and PEPPER to taste
4 lg. ripe TOMATOES, skinned and chopped

In a saucepan, cover potatoes and onions with water and cook until tender. Dice pork fine and fry until brown but not crisp. Add cooked pork and a little of the drippings to the potatoes and onions. Season to taste, then add chopped tomatoes. Simmer for 20 minutes.

Variation: Use 2 cups corn instead of tomatoes and cook the corn with the potatoes and onions.

Vegetable Beef Stew

3 med. ONIONS, sliced
3 Tbsp. VEGETABLE OIL
2 lbs. BEEF, cut in chunks
3 Tbsp. FLOUR
SALT and PEPPER to taste
1/4 tsp. THYME
1 cup CIDER
1 Tbsp. KETCHUP
3 lg. POTATOES, peeled and quartered
4 med. CARROTS, peeled and quartered

In a skillet, brown onions in hot oil; set aside. Add meat to skillet and brown. Combine flour, salt, pepper and thyme, and gradually add to the meat. Stir in cider and ketchup. Cover and simmer for 2 hours. Add potatoes and carrots to the meat. Cook for 30 minutes. Remove meat and vegetables to a platter and thicken drippings for gravy.

Dutch Oven Beef Stew

2 lbs. BEEF STEW MEAT
2 med. ONIONS, chopped
2 Tbsp. VEGETABLE OIL
2 1/2 cups HOT WATER
1 Tbsp. SUGAR
SALT and PEPPER to taste
1 can (16 oz.) whole TOMATOES, undrained
1 can (6 oz.) TOMATO PASTE
1 can (4 oz.) MUSHROOMS, sliced
1 cup thinly sliced CARROTS
2 CELERY STALKS, sliced
1/2 tsp. THYME
1/4 tsp. MARJORAM
1 BAY LEAF
2 Tbsp. FLOUR
1/4 cup COLD WATER

Cook beef and onions in oil in a Dutch oven until beef is brown. Stir in hot water, sugar, salt, pepper, tomatoes, tomato paste, and mushrooms. Heat to boiling, stirring occasionally; reduce heat. Cover and simmer, stirring occasionally, until beef is almost tender (about 1 1/2 hours). Add carrots, celery, thyme, marjoram, and bay leaf. Cover and simmer 30 minutes. Remove bay leaf. Blend flour and cold water; stir into stew mixture. Stir over heat until thick and bubbly.

World Champion Dutch Oven Cookoff

The Festival of the American West event held at the American West Heritage Center in Wellsville (just south of Logan) features championship teams from across the country participating in the World Champion Dutch Oven Cookoff.

Black Bean Soup

2 cans (15 oz. ea.) BLACK BEANS, drained
2 cans (15 oz. ea.) CHICKEN STOCK
1/2 cup chopped ONION
1 CARROT, chopped
1 stalk CELERY, chopped
SALT and PEPPER to taste
1/2 cup DRY SHERRY

Combine beans, chicken stock, onion, carrot and celery in a saucepan. Bring to a boil. Cover and simmer on low heat until vegetables are tender. Add salt and pepper, stir in the sherry.

Main Dishes

Raspberry-Apricot Glazed Cornish Hens

This recipe, created by Jeff Currier and Dick Hill, was a winning entry at the American West Festival Dutch Oven Cookoff which is held the first week of August each year.

American West Heritage Center—Wellsville

1 can (11.5 oz.) APRICOT NECTAR	1 Tbsp. VOLCANO®
1 cup RASPBERRY VINAIGRETTE	SEASONING
1 cup APRICOT JAM	SALT and PEPPER to taste
3-5 CORNISH HENS	SPRIGS of ROSEMARY

Inject apricot nectar into hens the night before cooking. Mix vinaigrette and jam together and set aside. Heat a 16-inch Dutch oven to 450°, using 22 charcoals on top and bottom. Wash hens and season with volcano seasoning, salt and pepper. Place two sprigs of rosemary inside each hen. Place hens in Dutch oven and cover with preheated lid. Cook for 45-60 minutes (as the hens brown, reduce heat to prevent burning.) Glaze hens with vinaigrette mixture about 20 minutes before done. Remove rosemary and discard. Glaze hens again before serving.

Baked Beef & Bean Casserole

1 1/2 lbs. GROUND BEEF
2 cans (15 oz. ea.) KIDNEY BEANS
2 cans (11 oz. ea.) PORK & BEANS
1 med. ONION, diced
1 sm. GREEN BELL PEPPER, chopped
3 Tbsp. BROWN SUGAR
CHILI PEPPER to taste
TABASCO® to taste
1 cup TOMATO SAUCE or BARBECUE SAUCE

Brown meat in a skillet and drain. Combine all ingredients in a casserole dish and bake at 350° for 30 to 45 minutes

---

Did You Know?

People from many backgrounds have played a part in Utah's growth. Indians, Mountain Men, religious groups and immigrants—all helped to build the Utah we know today.

Immigrants Beef Pie

1 med. ONION, chopped
1 Tbsp. OLIVE OIL
1 lb. GROUND BEEF
SALT and PEPPER to taste
1 can (14 oz.) GREEN BEANS, drained

1 can (10.75 oz.) TOMATO SOUP
5 POTATOES, peeled, boiled & mashed
1/2 cup warm MILK
1 EGG, beaten

Sauté onion in oil until translucent. Add meat and salt and pepper. Cook until meat is browned. Stir beans and soup into meat mixture; pour into a greased 1 1/2-quart casserole. In a bowl, combine mashed potatoes, milk and egg. Mix well. Spoon potato mixture onto meat mixture forming mounds on top. Bake 30 minutes at 350°.

Serves 6.

Stuffed Beef & Black Bean Tamale Pie

(See photo front and back covers)

National Cattlemen's Beef Association

1 lb. lean GROUND BEEF
1 pkg. (1 1/4 oz.) TACO SEASONING MIX
1 can (16 oz.) BLACK BEANS, rinsed, drained
1/2 cup WATER
1 can (8.75 oz.) WHOLE KERNEL CORN, very well drained
3/4 cup light dairy SOUR CREAM
3/4 cup shredded CHEDDAR CHEESE
1/3 cup thinly sliced GREEN ONIONS

Crust:
　1 pkg. (8 1/2 oz.) CORN MUFFIN MIX
　3/4 cup shredded CHEDDAR CHEESE
　3/4 cup light dairy SOUR CREAM
　1/2 cup thinly sliced GREEN ONIONS

Preheat oven to 400°. Heat large nonstick skillet over medium heat until hot. Add ground beef; brown 5 to 7 minutes, stirring occasionally. Pour off drippings. Stir in seasoning mix, beans and water. Bring to a boil; reduce heat. Simmer 5 minutes, stirring occasionally; set aside. In a medium bowl, combine crust ingredients, mixing just until dry ingredients are moistened. (Batter will be stiff.) Using a spoon dipped in water, spread slightly more than 1/2 of the batter onto bottom and up the sides of a 9-inch pie pan. Arrange corn over batter; top with beef mixture. Spoon remaining batter over beef, along outer edge of pie. Carefully spread batter toward center, leaving a 3-inch circle uncovered. Bake in a 400° oven for 23 to 25 minutes or until top is golden brown. To serve, dollop 3/4 cup sour cream over top; sprinkle with 3/4 cup cheese and 1/3 cup green onions. Cut into wedges.

Serves 4.

Joyce's Lasagna

Joyce Parrish (wife of Stanley B. Parrish, CEO and President, Salt
Lake Area Chamber of Commerce), Salt Lake City

1 lb. GROUND BEEF (cooked)
1 clove GARLIC, crushed
1 Tbsp. BASIL
1 Tsp. SALT
2 cups TOMATOES, chopped
2 cans (6 oz. ea.) TOMATO PASTE
3 cups small curd COTTAGE CHEESE
1/2 cup PARMESAN CHEESE
2 Tbsp. PARSLEY FLAKES
2 EGGS, beaten
1/2 tsp. PEPPER
1 pkg. (10 oz.) LASAGNA NOODLES, cooked
1 lb. MOZZARELLA CHEESE, grated

Combine the following ingredients together in a saucepan:
beef, garlic, basil, salt, tomatoes, and tomato paste. Stir until
well blended and allow to simmer over medium heat. Mix
together the cottage cheese, Parmesan cheese, parsley, eggs,
and pepper. Stir until well-blended. Set aside. In a 9 x 12
baking pan, place a layer of lasagna noodles, beef mixture,
cottage cheese mixture and top with mozzarella cheese. Continue alternating layers until all ingredients are used. Bake in
a 350° oven for 30 minutes. Let set for 10 minutes before
serving.

Barbecued Chicken

1/2 cup BARBECUE SAUCE
1/2 cup KETCHUP
1 Tbsp. LEMON JUICE
1/4 cup COOKING SHERRY
1 Tbsp. WORCESTERSHIRE SAUCE
Few drops TABASCO®
1 (2 1/2 lb.) CHICKEN,
    cut in quarters
2 Tbsp. BROWN SUGAR

Mix first six ingredients together. Put chicken in a flat
baking pan. Sprinkle brown sugar over meat. Pour barbecue
sauce mixture over meat. Bake at 375° for 1 to 1 1/2 hours.

Van Ausdal Dumplings

"These dumplings were served by my ancestors who came across the plains to Utah."

Bonnie Van Ausdal Hall—Santaquin

Boil **1 CHICKEN** in water until meat falls off bones. Debone chicken and return meat to broth. Add **SALT and PEPPER** to taste, plus **1 teaspoon SAGE**. In a separate bowl, combine **2 1/2 cups FLOUR** with **2 EGGS**. Add enough **WATER** to make pie dough consistency. Roll out on a floured surface and cut into rectangular strips about one inch wide. Bring chicken broth to a boil and drop in dough strips. Cook 15 minutes or until done.

Goblin Valley Chili

2 lbs. lean GROUND BEEF
1 tsp. SALT
2 cans (15 oz. ea.) CHILI, without beans
2 cans (16 oz. ea.) STEWED TOMATOES
2 cans (15 oz. ea.) RED KIDNEY BEANS
1 can (12 oz.) whole kernel CORN
1 lg. GREEN BELL PEPPER, diced
FRENCH BREAD

Form meat into 24 balls and brown well, turning several times. Spoon off excess fat. Stir in chili, tomatoes, kidney beans and corn. Heat slowly, stirring several times, to boiling. Simmer 15 minutes to season and blend flavors. Add green bell pepper. Ladle into serving bowls. Serve with French bread.

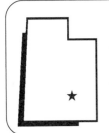

Goblin Valley State Park

At Goblin Valley State Park southwest of Green River, charge your imagination as you view this unusual rock display of thousands of colorful rock formations that resemble gnomes, goblins and spooks.

Curried Chicken with Vegetable Rice

A Pinch of Salt Lake —Junior League of Salt Lake City, Inc.,
Salt Lake City

Sauce:
- 1 cup HONEY
- 1/2 cup BUTTER
- 1/2 cup prepared MUSTARD
- 2 tsp. CURRY POWDER

3-4 whole CHICKEN BREASTS, skinned, boned and halved
1/4 cup chopped ONIONS
1/4 cup chopped GREEN BELL PEPPERS
1/2 cup chopped CELERY
4 Tbsp. BUTTER
1 can (8 oz.) sliced WATER CHESTNUTS, drained
1 cup sliced fresh MUSHROOMS
2 1/2 cups WATER
5 tsp. granulated CHICKEN BOUILLON
1 cup uncooked converted RICE

In a medium-size saucepan, bring sauce ingredients to a boil. Place chicken in a casserole dish and pour sauce over top. Bake, uncovered, for 45 minutes at 350°. Turn breasts and continue baking an additional 15-20 minutes. In a medium-size skillet, sauté onions, bell peppers and celery in butter. Add the water chestnuts and mushrooms. Bring 2 1/3 cups water to a boil in a large ovenproof saucepan. Add the bouillon, rice and vegetables. Bake, covered, for 45 minutes at 350°. Serve chicken over rice and vegetables.

Did You Know?

A monument in Salt Lake City honors Utah's State Bird, the sea gull, because sea gulls saved the settlers' harvest in 1848 by devouring swarms of crickets that had invaded the valley.

Salmon in Black & White

This recipe, created by Janet Froh, was a winning entry at the American West Festival Dutch Oven Cookoff which is held the first week of August each year.

4-6 fresh SALMON FILLETS, skin
   removed, cut into serving pieces
SALT to taste
1/2 cup WHITE SESAME SEEDS

1/2 cup BLACK SESAME
   SEEDS
2 Tbsp. OIL
LEMON JUICE

On waxed paper or saran, place a line of white sesame seeds about 2 inches wide and 10 inches long. Next to it, place an identical line of black sesame seeds. Lightly salt each fillet and dip them into the *Sesame Seed Coating.* Place fillets on the sesame seeds, pat gently, then turn carefully and pat again. Heat a 14-inch Dutch oven over 15 briquets. Lightly coat bottom with oil and heat. Place fillets in oven. Cover and add 20 briquets to lid. Cook approximately 20 minutes, depending on the thickness of the fillets. While cooking, occasionally sprinkle fillets with lemon juice. Remove fillets to serving dish.

Seasame Seed Coating

1/2 cup WHITE SESAME SEEDS
1 tsp. OIL
1/3 cup MAYONNAISE
1 tsp. ONION SALT
2 tsp. SALT

3 Tbsp. WHITE VINEGAR
1/3 cup LEMON JUICE
2 tsp. crushed RED PEPPER
1/4 tsp. LIQUID SMOKE
3 Tbsp. MILK

Combine seeds and oil in blender. Add balance of ingredients and blend until smooth. Refrigerate overnight to thicken and blend flavors.

Did You Know?

The Mormon Church maintains one of the largest collections of genealogical information in the world at The Family History Library in Salt Lake City.

Zucchini 'n Meatballs

1 pkg. BEEF BOUILLON	1 Tbsp. OIL
1/2 cup WATER	1/2 tsp. SALT
2 slices BREAD, crumbled	1 tsp. grated CHEDDAR CHEESE
2 tsp. chopped PARSLEY	1 can (8 oz.) TOMATO SAUCE
1 lb. GROUND BEEF or VEAL	4 med. ZUCCHINI, cut into
1 med. ONION, chopped	1/4" slices
1 clove GARLIC, minced	

Dissolve bouillon in water. Combine with bread, parsley and meat. Shape into 16 meatballs and refrigerate until firm. Sauté onion and garlic in oil until soft. Remove with a slotted spoon. Fry meatballs until brown on all sides, remove and set aside. In another skillet, place meatballs, onion, garlic and balance of ingredients. Bring to boil and then simmer, covered, about 10 minutes or until zucchini is tender.

Recreational opportunities abound in Utah: fishing, rock climbing, horseback riding, tours, historic railroad excursions, covered wagon treks, folklore fests, nature treks, archaeological tours, hiking, backpacking, mountain biking, golfing and skiing.

Meat-Stuffed Peppers

"This recipe was passed down to me by my grandmother."

Lynette Nelson—Salt Lake City

8 GREEN BELL PEPPERS	4 med. TOMATOES, chopped
1 sm. ONION, chopped	1 1/2 cups fresh CORN KERNELS
1 lb. GROUND BEEF	SALT and PEPPER to taste
2 tsp. FAT	buttered BREAD CRUMBS

Remove tops and seeds from bell peppers; parboil 5 minutes; drain. Brown onion and meat in hot fat; add tomatoes, corn and seasonings. Stuff peppers and top with buttered crumbs. Stand upright in greased baking dish. Add a small amount of water. Cover and bake at 350° for 1 hour.

Pizza Casserole

"You can use ground turkey or chicken instead of the beef in this recipe for a tasty variation."

Karen Anderson—Provo

1/2 cup chopped ONION
1/4 cup diced CELERY
1/4 cup chopped GREEN BELL
    PEPPER
1 Tbsp. OLIVE OIL
2 lbs. lean GROUND BEEF
SALT and PEPPER to taste
1 lg. POTATO, cubed

1 cup MUSHROOMS
1 can (8 oz.) TOMATO SAUCE
1 can (8 oz.) PIZZA SAUCE
1 cup WATER
PIZZA or BISCUIT DOUGH
Shredded MOZZARELLA
    CHEESE

In a large skillet, sauté onion, celery and pepper in oil. Add meat, potato, salt and pepper. Cook until meat has browned. Add mushrooms, tomato sauce, pizza sauce and water. Simmer until slightly thickened. Place pizza (or biscuit) dough that has been rolled out to a thickness of 1/4-inch in a large baking dish. Pour meat mixture over top. Sprinkle top with cheese. Bake in a preheated 400° oven for 15 minutes.

Green Chile & Turkey Enchiladas

Jerrie Finley—Salt Lake City

1/2 cup chopped ONIONS
1 can (4 oz.) diced GREEN CHILES
2 cups shredded cooked TURKEY
3 cups shredded CHEDDAR CHEESE

1 jar (24 oz.) GREEN CHILE
    ENCHILADA SAUCE
8 (6-inch) TORTILLAS
1/2 cup SOUR CREAM

Combine onion and chiles in a saucepan and sauté until onions are translucent. Add turkey, 1 cup of the cheese and the enchilada sauce; mix well. Spoon 1/2 cup of the turkey mixture down the center of each tortilla. Top with 1 tablespoon sour cream and roll up. Place tortillas seam side down in a baking dish. Pour remaining sauce over all and sprinkle with remaining cheese. Bake for 25-30 minutes at 350°.

Grandma's Chicken Casserole

"This recipe was given to me by grandmother Thomas—it has been in our family for over 100 years."

Ruby Dutson—Layton

3 CHICKEN BREASTS
1/2 cup BUTTER
1 can (10.75 oz.) CREAM OF CHICKEN SOUP
1 can (8 oz.) sliced WATER CHESTNUTS, drained
1/2 cup COOKING SAUTERNE
1 sm. GREEN BELL PEPPER, chopped
1/4 tsp. THYME
1 can (4.5 oz.) sliced MUSHROOMS, drained

Brown chicken breasts in butter and then arrange in a casserole dish (skin side up). Combine balance of ingredients and pour over top of chicken. Cover and bake at 375° for 1 hour.

Rancher's Beef Stroganoff

1/2 lb. fresh MUSHROOMS, sliced
1 lg. ONION, chopped
3 Tbsp. BUTTER, divided
2 lbs. ROUND STEAK
2 Tbsp. FLOUR
1 tsp. SALT
1 cup WATER
2 Tbsp. TOMATO PASTE
1 cube BEEF BOUILLON
1 cup WATER
1/2 cup SOUR CREAM

In a skillet, sauté mushrooms and onion in 2 Tbsp. butter; remove from pan. Cut steak into strips that are 2 1/2 inches long and 3/4 inch wide, removing fat and bone. Add remaining butter to pan and brown meat. Sprinkle flour and salt over meat, add water and tomato paste. Simmer until meat is tender (about 1 hour). Combine bouillon and water, add to meat mixture and bring to a boil. Reduce heat and stir in sour cream.

Serves 6-8.

Sesame Crusted Salmon

"Fresh seafood in Utah? That is what you will find at this seafood bistro featuring fresh oysters, seafood, meat and vegetarian dishes. This is a beautiful historic building."

Chef Mike Henson—350 Main-Seafood & Oyster Company, Park City

4 (6-8 oz.) SALMON FILLETS
1/2 cup SESAME SEEDS, toasted

1/4 cup OLIVE or SESAME OIL

Dredge salmon fillets in sesame seeds to coat completely. In a preheated pan on high heat, add oil to coat bottom of pan. Place fillets in pan and sear each side for a minute or so. Place in preheated 450° oven and roast for approximately 8-10 minutes depending on the thickness of the fillets. Fillets are done when meat flakes or separates when gently bent off the edge of a spatula, ideally until just medium rare. Serve with ***Pineapple Soy Glaze*** and ***Minted Cucumber Relish.***

Pineapple Soy Glaze

3 Tbsp. minced GARLIC
1/4 cup grated GINGER
1 cup SAKE (rice wine)
1/4 cup SESAME OIL
1/2 cup BROWN SUGAR

1 cup PINEAPPLE JUICE
1 cup SOY SAUCE
3 Tbsp. OYSTER SAUCE
1/2 cup CORNSTARCH
1/2 cup WARM WATER

In a saucepan, briefly sauté the garlic and gjinger in the sesame oil. Add brown sugar and pineapple juice and bring to a boil. Add soy and oyster sauces and allow to boil. Mix the cornstarch and water together. Add to boiling liquid, reduce heat to medium and allow mixture to thicken.

Minted Cucumber Relish

2 hothouse CUCUMBERS,
  skinned, seeded and diced
1/2 med. RED ONION, diced
3 Tbsp. chopped fresh MINT
  LEAVES

1 Tbsp. HONEY
1/4 cup OLIVE OIL
SALT and BLACK PEPPER
  to taste
3 Tbsp. RICE VINEGAR

Combine all ingredients together in a small bowl.

Bingham Lamb Chili

1 lb. lean GROUND LAMB	1 Tbsp. CHILI POWDER
1 cup chopped ONION	1/2 tsp. SALT
1 cup chopped CELERY	1/2 tsp. crushed OREGANO LEAVES
1 can (16 oz.) RED KIDNEY BEANS, undrained	1/4 tsp. crushed dry BASIL LEAVES
	2 tsp. SUGAR
1 can (16 oz.) TOMATO SAUCE	1 cup SALSA or PICANTE SAUCE

In a lightly oiled skillet, cook lamb, onion and celery over medium heat until lamb is no longer pink. Drain well; add remaining ingredients. Simmer on low for 30-45 minutes, stirring occasionally. Serve over **HOT RICE.**

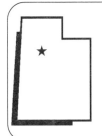

Greek Immigrants

Copper mining brought a large number of Greeks to the Bingham area during the 1890s. These immigrants brought with them a proud heritage. Greek Easter, one of their biggest feast day events, is celebrated with folk dances, colorful costumes and many traditional foods.

Apricot Chicken

"This recipe was developed to use our excess Aunty's Apricot Jam (A Meals on Wheels fund-raiser). It has become a favorite of everyone at the Senior Center."

Iantha Folkman—Brigham City Senior Center, Brigham City

1/2 cup AUNTY'S® APRICOT JAM
1/2 cup FRENCH or RUSSIAN DRESSING
1 env. ONION SOUP MIX
1 tsp. SOY SAUCE
4 CHICKEN BREASTS

Combine the first four ingredients together. Place chicken breasts in a casserole dish and spread jam mixture over top. Bake for 45 minutes at 375°. Serve over **COOKED RICE.**

Crown Roast
with Stuffed Mushrooms

This recipe, created by Kent Mayberry and Brian Terry, was a winning entry at the American West Festival Dutch Oven Cookoff which is held the first week of August each year.

American West Heritage Center, Wellsville

1 CROWN ROAST	1 Tbsp. BEEF BASE
PORK SEASONING	Juice of 2 LEMONS
1 gal. APPLE JUICE	12 lg. MUSHROOMS
1/2 tsp. ROSEMARY	24 PEARL ONIONS
1/2 tsp. SAGE	2 cubes BUTTER
1/2 tsp. THYME	2 bunches ASPARAGUS
SALT and PEPPER to taste	

Twelve hours before cooking, rub roast with pork seasoning and refrigerate. Let roast stand at room temperature one hour before cooking. In a saucepan, simmer and reduce apple juice by half. In a 15-inch Dutch oven, put half of the reduced apple juice, rosemary, sage, thyme, salt and pepper. Bring to a boil. Add roast and cook on medium fire (25 briquettes underneath, 20 on top) for 1 1/2 hours or until meat thermometer reaches 165°. Baste, adding remaining apple juice as needed. In a 12-inch Dutch oven, melt 2 cubes of butter, add beef base and lemon juice. Add mushrooms and onions and sauté until tender. Remove mushrooms and onions and steam asparagus until tender. Fill mushrooms with *Mushroom Stuffing*. Place meat on a serving platter and surround with the stuffed mushrooms, onions and asparagus. Serve.

Mushroom Stuffing

2 cubes BUTTER	1 pkg. SEASONED BREAD
1 RED ONION, chopped	CUBES
1 cup diced APPLES	1 Tbsp. CHICKEN BASE
1/4 tsp. ROSEMARY	1/4 tsp. THYME
1 tsp. SAGE	1 pkg. (4 oz.) sliced ALMONDS

Melt butter in Dutch oven. Add onion and apples and cook until caramelized. Add remaining ingredients and heat until bread cubes are brown.

Savory Sloppy Joes

1/2 cup chopped ONION	1 Tbsp. SALT
1/4 cup chopped CELERY	1 1/2 tsp. CHILI POWDER
1 Tbsp. COOKING OIL	1 tsp. WORCESTERSHIRE
1 1/2 lbs. GROUND BEEF	1/4 tsp. LIQUID SMOKE
2 cans (8 oz. ea.) TOMATO SAUCE	4 drops TABASCO®
1/2 cup WATER	1/4 lb. CHEDDAR CHEESE,
1/2 cup CHILI SAUCE	cubed
1/2 cup uncooked OATS	HAMBURGER BUNS, toasted

Cook onion and celery in hot oil until tender but not browned. Add beef and brown lightly. Stir in tomato sauce, water, chili sauce, oats, salt, chili powder, Worcestershire sauce, liquid smoke and Tabasco sauce. Cover and cook over low heat until slightly thickened (about 15 minutes). Stir occasionally. Fold in cubed cheese. When cheese has softened, combine and pour mixture over hamburger buns.

Serves 6-8.

Ogden

Situated at the confluence of the Weber and Ogden rivers, this city was named for Peter Skene Ogden, an early fur trapper. The Golden Spike, driven near Ogden in May, 1869 commemorated the completion of the first transcontinental railroad system.

Golden Tuna Cakes

2 slices of BREAD	1/2 tsp. DRY MUSTARD
1 can (6.5 oz.) TUNA	1/4 tsp. SALT
1 EGG	1 Tbsp. OLIVE OIL
1 tsp. WORCESTERSHIRE SAUCE	DILL RELISH

Remove crust from bread and tear into small pieces. Mix together bread, tuna, egg, worcestershire sauce, mustard, and salt. Shape mixture into 3 firm patties, each about 1/2 inch thick. Fry patties in oil over medium heat until golden brown. Serve with dill relish on the side.

Stuffed Pork Chops

1 lg. ONION, finely chopped
1/2 cup finely chopped CELERY
1/4 cup chopped NUTS
2 Tbsp. BUTTER
3/4 cup soft, fresh BREADCRUMBS
1/4 cup chopped PARSLEY
1/8 tsp. grated NUTMEG

1 EGG, lightly beaten
SALT and PEPPER
   to taste
6 double loin PORK CHOPS
   with pockets
1 cup BEEF STOCK

Preheat oven to 350°. Sauté the onion, celery and nuts in the butter until the onion is soft. Remove from heat. Add the bread crumbs, parsley, nutmeg, egg, salt and pepper to the onion mixture. Mix well. Stuff pork chops with the bread crumb mixture. Place the chops in a shallow baking dish, cover with foil and bake for about one hour, turning after 30 minutes. Uncover and continue baking about 30 more minutes until well browned. Remove chops and keep warm. For sauce: Drain drippings from the pan; add beef stock and heat, while scraping loose any browned particles that cling to the pan. Pour the sauce around the chops.

Shepherd's Beef Pie

"This recipe was a favorite for church suppers as well as family get-togethers."

Maria Harnell—Bountiful

4 cups leftover cooked BEEF, finely chopped
2 cups leftover GRAVY
3 cups VEGETABLES, fresh cooked or leftovers
1 med. ONION, chopped
1 EGG
SALT and PEPPER to taste
MASHED POTATOES
FAT (substitute with vegetable oil, if desired)

Mix all ingredients together except potatoes and fat and place in a buttered baking dish. Cover surface of mixture with mashed potatoes and dot with fat. Bake in a 400° oven until heated through and potatoes are golden brown.

Cache Valley Tacos

1 whole CHICKEN, cut in half
2 ONIONS, chopped
1 can (7 oz.) diced GREEN CHILES
12 CORN TORTILLAS
1 1/2 lbs. LONGHORN CHEESE, shredded
3 TOMATOES, diced
1/2 head LETTUCE, shredded
1 AVOCADO, sliced

Place chicken in a large saucepan and cover with water. Bring to a boil, then reduce heat to medium and cook for 45 minutes. Remove meat from bones and shred. Combine chicken meat with onions and green chiles. Fry corn tortillas in a small amount of oil until brown, but still pliable. Fill with meat mixture; top with cheese, tomatoes, lettuce and avocado slice and fold in half.

Cache Valley Sugar Beets

The first beet sugar was produced in Utah at the Lehi factory of the Utah Sugar company in 1891. By 1900, the Utah Sugar Company and the Ogden Sugar Company produced enough sugar to fulfill all of Utah's needs.

Cottonwood Cornish Hens

4 CORNISH GAME HENS
SALT and PEPPER to taste
1/2 cup FLOUR
2 Tbsp. OLIVE OIL

6 Tbsp. BUTTER, divided
1 1/2 cups CHICKEN BROTH
2 Tbsp. LEMON JUICE
4 Tbsp. PARSLEY

Rinse hens and pat dry. Tie legs together and sprinkle with salt, pepper and flour. In a large pot, heat oil and 2 tablespoons butter over medium heat and brown hens on all sides (5 to 7 minutes). Reduce heat to low, cover and cook 20 to 30 minutes. Put hens on serving platter and keep warm. Add broth to pot and reduce until syrupy. Whisk in 4 tablespoons butter, remove from heat, add lemon and parsley, pour over hens.

Serves 4.

Provo Bean & Biscuit Casserole

1/2 cup chopped ONION
3/4 cup chopped GREEN BELL PEPPER
2 Tbsp. BUTTER or MARGARINE
1 lb. HOT DOGS, sliced
1 can (16 oz.) PORK & BEANS
1/3 cup CHILI SAUCE
1/3 cup KETCHUP
1-2 Tbsp. BROWN SUGAR, firmly packed
1 can (8 oz.) BUTTERMILK BISCUITS
3/4 cup shredded CHEDDAR CHEESE
1/2 cup crushed CORN CHIPS
3 Tbsp. grated ROMANO or PARMESAN CHEESE
BUTTER to taste

In large skillet, sauté onion and bell pepper in 1 tablespoon butter until tender. Stir in hot dogs, beans, chili sauce and ketchup (for a sweeter flavor, add brown sugar). Simmer two minutes. Spoon hot mixture into ungreased 12 x 8 pan. Separate biscuit dough into 10 biscuits. Pull each biscuit apart and arrange half of them over the hot meat mixture. Sprinkle with cheddar cheese. Arrange remaining biscuits on top. Combine corn chips and cheese; sprinkle over biscuits. Dot biscuits with butter. Bake at 375° for 20 to 25 minutes until biscuits are golden brown.

Serves 6-8.

Provo

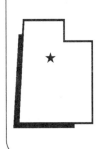

Settled in 1849 by a colony from Salt Lake City, this city was named after Etienne Provost, a French-Canadian who explored the area. Provo is home to Brigham Young University, which has a 634-acre campus and is dominated by the 112-foot Centennial Carillon Tower with its 52 bells that ring at intervals throughout the day.

Pacific Rim Glazed Flank Steak

Winner of the National Beef Cook-Off, Sponsored by American National Cattle Women, Inc., Utah Cattle Women and the Utah Beef Council.

Chris Freymuller—Salt Lake City

1 (1-1 1/2 lb.) BEEF FLANK STEAK

Marinade:
    1 cup prepared TERIYAKI MARINADE
    1/2 cup chopped ONION
    1/3 cup HONEY
    1/3 cup fresh ORANGE JUICE
    1 Tbsp. chopped fresh ROSEMARY
    1 Tbsp. dark SESAME OIL
    1 clove GARLIC, crushed
    PEPPER to taste

In a medium shallow dish, combine marinade ingredients and whisk until blended. Remove and reserve 3/4 cup for basting. With a sharp knife, lightly score both sides of beef steak in a crisscross pattern. Place steak in remaining marinade in dish, turning to coat. Cover and marinate in refrigerator for 30 minutes, turning once. Remove steak from marinade; discard marinade. Place steak on grid over medium, ash-covered coals. Grill, uncovered, 17 to 21 minutes for medium rare to medium doneness, basting occasionally with reserved marinade and turning once. Place remaining basting marinade in small saucepan; bring to a boil. Carve steak diagonally across the grain into thin slices; arrange on platter. Spoon hot marinade over beef.

Serves 4-6.

Did You Know?

Salt Lake City's wide streets are the result of the pioneers' need to be able to turn around a team of oxen and a covered wagon.

Spaghettini with Prosciutto & Peas

in a Roasted Tomato and Fennel Broth

Chef Todd Gardiner—Iron Blossom Lodge, Wildflower Restaurant, Snowbird

8 ripe ROMA TOMATOES
1 bud FENNEL
2 Tbsp. extra virgin OLIVE OIL, divided
SALT and PEPPER to taste
1/4 lb. diced PROSCIUTTO di PARMA
1/4 lb. fresh SUGAR SNAP PEAS
1 lb. SPAGHETTINI cooked, drained and cooled
ITALIAN PARSLEY
Freshly ground ASIAGO CHEESE

Under a broiler or over a charcoal grill, cook whole tomatoes until the skin begins to blacken. Meanwhile, quarter fennel and remove core. Rub with one half tablespoon oil and sprinkle with salt and pepper. Place in a preheated 350° oven for 15-20 minutes or until fennel begins to soften. When fennel has softened, place in a blender with the tomatoes and one table-spoonful oil. Blend to a smooth sauce. Adjust consistency with a little water if necessary. Place prosciutto and peas in a hot sauté pan and cook until the peas just begin to soften. Add sauce, one half tablespoon oil and spaghettini. Toss to coat pasta with sauce. Arrange on serving dishes; garnish with parsley and Asiago cheese.

Serves 4-6.

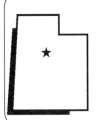

Snowbird/Alta Area

In 1865, when silver was discovered in this Wasatch Mountain area, Alta became a raucous mining town of over 5,000 overnight. Today, this entire area is world famous as a popular ski locale.

Cache Valley Cheese Soufflé

"Some people are surprised to learn that Utah is home to acres of lush dairyland, much of it in Cache Valley, in northern Utah. It's home to two of the nation's largest Swiss cheese factories—Gossner's Foods and Cache Valley Cheese."

Always In Season, Junior League of Salt Lake City, Inc., Salt Lake City

1/4 cup FLOUR
3 Tbsp. melted BUTTER
1 cup (scant) MILK
3/4 cup shredded CHEDDAR CHEESE
SALT and CAYENNE to taste
3 EGG YOLKS
4 EGG WHITES

Blend the flour in the butter in a saucepan. Cook until bubbly, stirring constantly. Stir in the milk. Cook until thickened, stirring constantly. Add the cheese, stirring until melted. Remove from heat and season with salt and cayenne. Stir a small amount of the hot mixture into the egg yolks and then blend the yolks into the hot mixture. Beat the egg whites until stiff peaks form. Add 1 tablespoon of the cooked mixture to the egg whites and blend. Fold the remainder of the egg whites gently into the cooked mixture. Adjust the seasonings. Spoon into a buttered and floured 5 to 6-inch soufflé dish. Place dish in a preheated 425° oven. Reduce the oven temperature to 400°. Bake for 20 to 25 minutes or until soufflé is brown and puffed but still moist in the center.

Serves 4.

Did You Know?

The Great Salt Lake's salinity varies from 15 to 25 percent making it approximately 6 times saltier than the ocean. Only blue-green algae and brine shrimp can survive in this lake's waters.

Spaghetti Pie

Sharon Kunzler's prize-winning recipe of the 1997
Utah Beef Producer Cook-Off.

Utah Cattle Women & Utah Beef Council, Salt Lake City

2 lbs. GROUND BEEF	1 can (6 oz.) MUSHROOMS,
SALT to taste	sliced
1 sm. ONION, diced	1 pkg. (12 oz.) SPAGHETTI
3 cans (8 oz. ea.) TOMATO	1 EGG
SAUCE	1 can (2 oz.) OLIVES, drained
1 1/2 cups WATER	and sliced
2 Tbsp. SUGAR	3/4 cup PARMESAN CHEESE
2 Tbsp. VINEGAR	1/2 cup MARGARINE
2 pkgs. (1.5 oz. ea.) SCHILLING®	1/2 lb. MONTEREY JACK
SPAGHETTI SAUCE MIX	CHEESE, shredded

Brown and lightly salt ground beef. Combine onion, tomato sauce, water, sugar, vinegar, spaghetti sauce mix and mushrooms with beef and simmer. In a separate pan, cook spaghetti according to package directions; drain and rinse in hot water. Place spaghetti in a bowl and add egg, olives, Parmesan cheese (reserve some for topping) and margarine. Mix well.

Line the sides and bottom of a 9 x 13 baking pan with spaghetti mixture. Pour meat mixture over center of spaghetti and up over the sides. Top with shredded cheese and sprinkle with reserved Parmesan cheese. Bake at 325° for 25-30 minutes. Serve with garlic bread.

Serves 6-8.

Moab

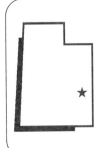

Zane Grey used Moab and the surrounding area as the setting for many of his novels. Moab has served as the background for many movies, including, "Thelma and Louise", "City Slickers II" and "Geronimo!" Moab was also a familiar city to Butch Cassidy's Wild Bunch.

Coriander Seared Ahi

Log Haven Restaurant was recently voted "Best Salt Lake City Restaurant" by Salt Lake City Magazine. It is serenely nestled in the heart of the Wasatch National Forest, among pines, waterfalls and wildflowers. The Deseret News calls it an "amazing gastronomical getaway."

Chef David Jones—Log Haven Restaurant, Salt Lake City

2 lbs. SASHIMI GRADE AHI

Remove skin from ahi and cut into four pieces of approximately 7-8 ounces each. Cut into triangles or cylinders. Wrap in plastic or butcher paper and set aside in refrigerator.

Coriander Rub:
   2/3 cup CLARIFIED BUTTER
   2 Tbsp. SESAME OIL
   1/2 bunch CILANTRO, finely chopped
   1 tsp. freshly ground CORIANDER
   1/2 tsp. freshly ground BLACK PEPPER
   1/2 tsp. freshly ground WHITE PEPPER
   1/4 tsp. CAYENNE PEPPER
   1 tsp. GARLIC POWDER
   1 tsp. ONION POWDER
   1 tsp. chopped LEMON THYME
   1 1/2 tsp. SALT
   1/2 tsp. SUGAR
   1 Tbsp. SOY SAUCE

To end up with 2/3 cup of clarified butter, start with about a pound of butter. Combine all ingredients together and set aside at room temperature.

Pink Guava-Lime Sauce:
   **2 cups PINK GUAVA PURÉE (guava juice may
      be substituted. Reduce by 1/2)**
   2 cups CRANBERRY JUICE
   1/2 cup LIME JUICE
   1/8 cup LEMON JUICE
   2 Tbsp. GINGER JUICE

(Continued next page)

Coriander Seared Ahi (continued)

1/2 cup SUGAR, or to taste
SALT and WHITE PEPPER to taste

Place the guava purée in a saucepan. Add juices. Reduce by about 1/2 until it reaches sauce consistency. Once sauce is reduced, add sugar to taste. Amount of sugar will vary depending on the ripeness of the guava. Be sure this sauce is not too tart or too sweet. Finish with salt and pepper. Set aside.

Mango Salsa:
 1 MANGO, finely diced
 2 KIWI, finely diced
 1 sm. MAUI or VIDALIA ONION, finely diced
 1-2 RED JALAPEÑO PEPPERS
 1/4-1/3 bunch (to taste) CILANTRO, finely diced
 1 Tbsp. finely chopped PICKLED GINGER
 LIME JUICE, to taste
 SALT and PEPPER to taste

Combine all ingredients in a glass bowl and refrigerate.

Rice Roll:
 2 bunches GREEN ONIONS, GRILLED
 2 sheets TOASTED NORI
 1/2 cup MACADAMIA NUTS, toasted

Sauté or grill the green onions, using mostly the whites. Set the nori, green onions and macadamia nuts aside.

Sushi Rice:
 2 1/2 cups CAL ROSE® RICE
 3 1/4 cups WATER
 1/2 cup SWEET GINGER RICE VINEGAR
 3 Tbsp. SUGAR
 1 Tbsp. SALT

It is very important to clean the Cal-Rose rice by rinsing in lukewarm water about 5 times. End up with a clear water in this rinsing procedure. Let rice sit in a saucepan for 1/2 hour after draining. The residual water from the rinsing will soften the rice kernels. Add water; bring to a boil and then reduce to

(Continued next page)

Coriander Seared Ahi (continued)

a simmer. Cook for about 15 minutes, or until most of the water has evaporated or been absorbed by the rice. Cover rice with a damp towel or lid and keep in a warm place for 15 minutes or until it reaches room temperature. In a separate bowl, mix the vinegar, sugar and salt. Mix the sushi seasoning into the rice, cover bowl with a damp towel and place in refrigerator.

Soy Glaze:
   1 cup SAKE
   1/2 cup SOY SAUCE
   2 cups SUGAR
   2 tsp. BUTTER
   Dash of LEMON JUICE

Bring sake and soy sauce to a boil. Stir in sugar. Mixture should be of a teriyaki sauce consistency. Add more sugar if needed to balance the salt in the soy sauce. Stir in butter and lemon juice and mix until butter has melted. Pour into a squirt bottle or leave, covered, in a warm place.

Assembly:

Use a sushi roller (bamboo slotted). Place plastic wrap on top of sushi roller. Divide sushi rice into two parts. Take one portion and spread out evenly (by hand) on plastic. Place a sheet of toasted nori on top of the rice. Arrange green onions and toasted macadamia nuts in the center of the sushi roll and roll up. Remove from sushi roller, wrap in plastic wrap and refrigerate. Repeat process for the second rice roll.

Five minutes before starting ahi:

Cut rice rolls in half and fry in peanut oil until golden brown on outside. Slice and arrange on serving plate.

Preparing the ahi:

Dredge ahi through coriander rub. Place in a white hot iron skillet. Sear approximately 1 1/2 minutes on each side. Remove from pan and let sit for a minute. Slice and arrange ahi on serving plates and garnish as desired.

Side Dishes

Mom's Celery Casserole

Rachel is a former Miss Utah USA.

Rachel Rasmussen—Ogden

6 cups sliced CELERY
2 cans (10.75 oz. ea.) CREAM OF CHICKEN SOUP
1 can (8 oz.) WATER CHESTNUTS, diced
2 Tbsp. PIMENTO
1/2 cup slivered ALMONDS
3/4 cup MELTED BUTTER
1 1/4 cups crushed NABISCO® ONION CRACKERS

In a saucepan, cover celery with water and boil for 4 minutes; drain. Add chicken soup, water chestnuts, and pimento to saucepan. In a skillet, sauté almonds in butter; add onion crackers. Place celery mixture in a casserole dish, sprinkle cracker mixture over top. Bake for 20 minutes at 350°.

Broccoli & Stuffing Mix

1 EGG
1 pkg. (10 oz.) frozen chopped BROCCOLI, thawed
1 can (15 oz.) CREAM-STYLE CORN
1 Tbsp. grated ONION
SALT and PEPPER to taste
3 Tbsp. BUTTER or MARGARINE
1 cup HERB SEASONED STUFFING MIX

In mixing bowl, combine egg, broccoli, corn, onion, salt and pepper. In a small saucepan, melt butter or margarine; add herb buttered stuffing mix and toss to coat. Stir 3-4 cups of the buttered stuffing mix into the vegetable mixture. Turn into an ungreased one-quart casserole dish. Sprinkle with remaining stuffing mix. Bake, uncovered, in a 350° oven 30 to 40 minutes.

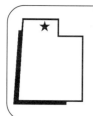

Logan

The Jardine Juniper, believed to be the oldest living juniper on our planet (1,500 years old) can be found near Logan. Also, to the west are the Wellsville Mountains, said to be the world's tallest montains on the narrowest base.

Dutch Oven-Style Microwaved Potatoes

Becky Lowe—Utah State University Home Economics Extension, Salt Lake City

6 med. BAKING POTATOES
6 strips BACON, fried
 until crisp

1 ONION, sliced into rings
SALT and PEPPER to taste

Peel or scrub potatoes and then slice into 1/4-inch slices (or 1-inch cubes). Layer bacon, onion and then potatoes in a microwaveable dish; sprinkle with salt and pepper. Cook on HIGH for 15 minutes 2-3 minutes or until potatoes are tender.

Green Chile & Corn Pie

1 cup BUTTER or MARGARINE
1 cup SUGAR
4 EGGS, whipped
1 can (4 oz.) diced GREEN CHILES
1 can (15 oz.) CREAM-STYLE CORN
1/2 cup shredded LONGHORN CHEDDAR CHEESE
1/2 cup shredded MONTEREY JACK CHEESE
1 cup FLOUR
1 cup YELLOW CORNMEAL
4 tsp. BAKING POWDER
pinch of SALT

Cream together the butter and sugar. Mix eggs slowly into the butter mixture, stirring constantly. Add chiles, creamed corn and cheeses. In a separate bowl, sift together the flour, corn meal, baking powder and salt. Blend dry ingredients into the corn mixture. Pour into a greased and floured 8 x 12 baking dish and bake at 300° for 1 hour.

Serves 12.

Pine Nut Potato Casserole

6 med. POTATOES, unpeeled
1/4 cup PINE NUTS
1 ctn. (12 oz.) small-curd
   COTTAGE CHEESE
1/2 cup SOUR CREAM
1/4 cup ONION, finely minced
SALT and PEPPER to taste
BUTTER or MARGARINE
TOASTED ALMONDS

Dice and boil potatoes in a large pot until tender. Place the pine nuts in a small skillet and toast over medium-high heat, stirring constantly with a wooden spoon. Drain potatoes well and add pine nuts. Add cottage cheese, sour cream, onion, and salt and pepper to potato mixture. Mash with an electric beater until creamy. (Adjust the proportions of sour cream and cottage cheese to suit taste and texture). Spoon potato mixture into a lightly buttered casserole dish. Sprinkle toasted almonds on top. Dot with butter. Bake, uncovered, at 350° for 30 minutes.

Green Chile Rice

3 1/2 cups RICE, cooked
1 can (4 oz.) diced GREEN CHILES
1 can (4 oz.) PIMENTOS, chopped
1 tsp. SALT
1 cup SOUR CREAM
4 oz. CHEDDAR CHEESE, grated
4 oz. MONTEREY JACK CHEESE, grated

Cook rice according to directions. Cut green chiles and pimentos into bite size pieces. Next, combine salt and sour cream. Add cheeses and stir until blended. Spread mixture into pre-greased 9 x 9 baking pan and bake in preheated oven at 350° for 45 minutes.

Hovenweep Corn Fritters

1/2 cup FLOUR
1/2 tsp. BAKING POWDER
1/2 tsp. SALT
PAPRIKA

1 cup canned CORN, drained
1 EGG, separated
OIL for frying

Combine first four ingredients together. Add corn to mixture and stir well. Add beaten egg yolk and stir. Fold in stiffly beaten egg white. Drop fritters into hot oil and fry until golden brown. Serve with syrup of choice.

Hovenweep
National Monument

Hovenweep National Monument is an ancient Pueblo ruin that lies on the far eastern border of Utah. The ruins of many-roomed pueblos, small cliff dwellings and towers are scattered over the canyon slopes. Hovenweep is a Ute Indian word which means "deserted valley".

Mashed Potatoes & Cheese Casserole

5 med. whole POTATOES, boiled and peeled
1 Tbsp. BUTTER, melted
GARLIC POWDER, light sprinkle
5 dashes TABASCO®
1 Tbsp. SESAME SEEDS
1 Tbsp. grated ONION
1 1/2 cups sm. curd COTTAGE CHEESE
1 1/3 cups grated PARMESAN CHEESE
4 EGGS, beaten

Topping:
  PARMESAN CHEESE
  CORNFLAKES, crushed

Coarsely chop potatoes into a large mixing bowl and add melted butter, garlic powder, Tabasco sauce, sesame seeds and onion. Mash thoroughly with potato masher. Add cottage cheese, Parmesan cheese and eggs. Combine ingredients thoroughly. Turn potato mixture into a greased, shallow baking dish and spread evenly. Sprinkle top with mixture of crushed cornflakes and Parmesan cheese. Bake at 350° for 30 minutes.

Spinach Rice Bake

1 pkg. (10 oz.) chopped
    frozen SPINACH
1 cup cooked RICE
2 EGGS, slightly beaten
2 Tbsp. BUTTER
1/3 cup MILK
2 Tbsp. chopped ONION
1/2 tsp. WORCESTERSHIRE
    SAUCE
1 tsp. SALT
1/4 tsp. THYME

Cook spinach; drain well. Combine remaining ingredients, mix well and add to spinach. Pour spinach mixture into 9-inch square baking dish. Bake at 350° for 20 to 25 minutes or until knife comes out clean.

Serves 6-8.

Mountain Beans

1 lb. CANADIAN BACON	1/4 tsp. MARJORAM
1/2 cup diced ONION	1/4 tsp. SALT
1 clove GARLIC, minced	1 tsp. DRY MUSTARD
2 cans (16 oz. ea.) PORK & BEANS	1/2 cup MOLASSES
2 tsp. liquid GRAVY MIX	

Cut Canadian bacon into 1/4-inch thick slices then into large chunks. Cook in skillet until brown and slightly crisp. Add onion and garlic and cook until just tender, about 5 minutes. Add beans, gravy mix, marjoram, salt and mustard. Mix in molasses. Cover, cook over low heat for 30 minutes. Remove cover and continue cooking 15 minutes longer, stirring occasionally.

Serves 4-6.

Salt Lake Sweet Potatoes

2 cans (16 oz. ea.) SWEET POTATOES, drained and mashed
1 can (9 oz.) sliced PINEAPPLE, reserve juice
2 APPLES, diced
1 can WATER CHESTNUTS, chopped

Place sweet potatoes in a large bowl. Pour half of ***Pineapple Syrup*** (see below) into sweet potatoes and mash. Add apples and water chestnuts to potatoes and combine. Line a buttered casserole dish with pineapple rings. Add potato mixture; pour remaining syrup over mixture. Bake at 350° for 45 minutes.

Serves 9-12.

Pineapple Syrup

3 Tbsp. BUTTER	1 1/2 tsp. GINGER
1 1/2 tsp. CINNAMON	reserved PINEAPPLE JUICE
1 JIGGER RUM	

Melt butter in skillet. Add cinnamon, rum, ginger and remaining pineapple syrup. Stir until mixed well.

Ranch-Style Beans

2 lbs. dry PINTO BEANS
2 Tbsp. SALT
2 lg. ONIONS, diced
4 cloves GARLIC, diced
1 can (4 oz.) diced GREEN CHILES
1 can (12 oz.) TACO SAUCE
1 can (16 oz.) crushed TOMATOES
1/2 tsp. BLACK PEPPER
1/2 tsp. CUMIN SEED

Soak pinto beans in cold water overnight. Drain; wash, and cover with about 2 inches of water, add salt and boil over moderate heat for one hour, adding water if needed. Add balance of ingredients. Cook over reduced heat until beans are tender (1 to 1 1/2 hours).

Serves 10.

Variation: This recipe may be easily converted into a delicious chili con carne by adding 2 pounds of chopped beef, sautéed until brown with a chopped onion. Add to beans after the first hour of cooking.

Did You Know?

John A. Widtsoe helped develop the first successful dry farming methods in the United States. San Juan County was the site of one of the first of these experimental farms.

Potato Puffs

"I found this recipe in an old cookbook that belonged to my great-grandmother."

Martha Vance—Provo

1 pint MASHED POTATOES
1 level tsp. BAKING POWDER
1 cup FLOUR

2 EGGS
SALT to taste
FAT for cooking

Combine all ingredients and drop from a tablespoon into hot fat. Cook until browned.

Roasted Red New Potatoes with Lemon

3 lbs. sm. RED NEW POTATOES, quartered
SALT and PEPPER to taste
1/4 cup UNSALTED BUTTER
1/4 cup OLIVE OIL
6 Tbsp. fresh LEMON JUICE
2 tsp. crumbled dried THYME
1 Tbsp. grated LEMON PEEL
3 Tbsp. fresh PARSLEY, minced

Place potatoes in a large, shallow, greased, oven-proof casserole dish. Season with salt and pepper to taste. Melt butter with oil in a small heavy saucepan over medium heat. Add lemon juice. Pour over potatoes and toss well. Sprinkle potatoes with thyme. Bake in a 350° oven for 1 hour. Add lemon peel and toss to coat potatoes. Continue baking until potatoes are tender and deep golden-brown; about 15 minutes. Sprinkle potatoes with minced parsley and serve.

For variation: delete the grated lemon peel and lemon juice and substitute with fresh whole mushrooms and onions.

San Juan Jalapeño Cabbage

OLIVE OIL
1 Tbsp. BLACK MUSTARD SEEDS
1 JALAPEÑO PEPPER, seeded and diced
1/2 sm. ONION, sliced
1 sm. RED CABBAGE, shredded
1 sm. GREEN CABBAGE, shredded

Heat a large skillet and coat with olive oil; add mustard seeds. When the seeds start to pop, put in the jalapeño pepper, onion, and equal portions of green and red cabbage. Toss until the cabbage is wilted and coated with oil, about 5 minutes.

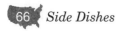

Beehive Barbeque Sauce

1/4 cup chopped ONIONS	1 GREEN BELL PEPPER, chopped
1/4 cup chopped CELERY	1 jar (12 oz.) CHILI SAUCE
2 Tbsp. OLIVE OIL	1 Tbsp. WORCESTERSHIRE
1/2 Tbsp. PAPRIKA	SAUCE
1 tsp. SALT	3 drops TABASCO® SAUCE
1/2 LEMON, juiced	1/2 cup HONEY
1/4 cup BROWN SUGAR	1/4 cup WATER
1/4 cup VINEGAR	1 Tbsp. MUSTARD

Sauté onions and celery in oil and add the remaining ingredients in the order given. Simmer 30 minutes. Pour over browned meat, fish or poultry and bake as directed.

Makes 1 quart.

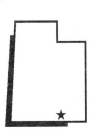

Rainbow Bridge National Monument

Located in the Glen Canyon National Recreation Area, Rainbow Bridge is the largest known natural bridge in the world. It stands 309 feet above the bottom of a gorge, and has a 278-foot span. The bridge is listed as a natural wonder of the world. The area was established as a national monument in 1910.

Calabaza con Queso
(Squash with Cheese)

2 lbs. fresh ZUCCHINI or SUMMER SQUASH
1/2 lb. CHEDDAR CHEESE, grated
1 can (4 oz.) diced GREEN CHILES

Wash and then cut squash into small pieces. Boil until tender in salted water (about 15 minutes). Drain. Layer squash in a greased casserole dish. Sprinkle with half of the diced chile and half of the cheese. Repeat layers. Heat in a 400° oven until cheese melts and forms a sauce.

Swiss Sweet & Sour Red Cabbage

LaRee P. Hunt & Leah Probst Godfry

1 Tbsp. BUTTER
1 ONION, cubed
1 GRANNY SMITH or CORTLAND APPLE, cubed
1 sm. head RED CABBAGE, shredded
1 1/2 cups WATER
1/2 cup VINEGAR
SALT and PEPPER to taste
6 WHOLE CLOVES
1 tsp. SUGAR

In a skillet, melt butter; add onion and apple and sauté until onion is translucent. Add remaining ingredients and simmer for one hour.

Midway Boosters and Swiss Days

These two Swiss recipes are from the Midway Boosters "Heritage Cookbook," introduced at Swiss Days 2001. Swiss Days date back to the late 1940s when local farmers and ranchers got together for a celebration of the fall harvest. The Midway Boosters, who organize this event, use the proceeds to provide for many projects and improvements to Midway City facilities and programs.

Rosti

Lucy Thompson

6 lg. unpeeled POTATOES   **1 med. ONION, grated**
1/2 lb. BACON, cubed   **1/2 lb. sliced SWISS CHEESE**

Boil potatoes in salted water until just tender; cool, peel and grate. In a skillet, fry bacon until crisp; remove and set aside. Add onion and sauté until translucent. Add potatoes, stir and then press into a cake Brown lightly on both sides. Place Swiss cheese on one half and fold over. Continue cooking until both sides are brown and crisp.

 *Side Dishes*

San Juan County Fry Bread

"Fifty-four percent of the population in San Juan County is made up of Navajo Indians. This bread is a mainstay in their diet. The Navajos also make tacos with this dough."

Becky Low—Utah State University Extension, Salt Lake City

3-5 cups FLOUR
2 tsp. SALT
2 Tbsp. BAKING POWDER

2 cups WATER
OIL, for frying

Heat 1 inch of oil in a deep skillet to 375°. Combine 2 cups flour, salt, baking powder and water. Mix well. Stir in enough more flour to make a soft dough. Turn dough out on a floured surface and knead until smooth and elastic. Pinch off about a 3-inch ball of dough. Flatten dough with hands and stretch into a 7-8-inch circle about 1/4-inch thick. Fry in hot oil until light golden brown, turn and brown the other side. Drain on paper towels. Serve with stew (mutton is best), jam, jelly, or with honey and butter.

Pioneer Whole-Wheat Bread

"Threshing day was almost as exciting as the 4th of July in the early days. Men would go from farm to farm, helping their neighbors and looking forward to a lavish, noon-day feast at the field owner's home."

Heritage Cookbook—Junior League of Salt Lake City, Inc., Salt Lake City

1 pkg. dry YEAST
1/4 cup WARM WATER
2 cups MILK
1/4 cup HONEY

2 Tbsp. VEGETABLE OIL
3/4 tsp. SALT
4 cups WHOLE-WHEAT
  FLOUR, unsifted

Soak yeast in warm water for 10 minutes. Scald milk, cool and mix with honey, vegetable oil and salt. Stir in yeast and whole-wheat flour. Mix well. Knead until easy to handle. Let rise 15 minutes. Divide and put into two small greased loaf pans and bake at 350° for 45 minutes.

Blueberry-Pumpkin Muffins

1 2/3 cups FLOUR
1 tsp. BAKING SODA
1/2 tsp. SALT
1 tsp. CINNAMON
1/2 tsp. ALLSPICE
1 cup COOKED PUMPKIN
1/4 cup EVAPORATED MILK

1/3 cup BUTTER
1 cup firmly packed LIGHT
  BROWN SUGAR
1 EGG
1 cup BLUEBERRIES
1 Tbsp. FLOUR

Combine flour, soda, salt, cinnamon and allspice together in a mixing bowl; stir and set aside. Mix pumpkin and evaporated milk until blended and set aside. Cream butter and sugar together in large mixing bowl. Add egg to sugar mixture and blend until mixture is fluffy. Add flour mixture to butter mixture, alternating with pumpkin mixture, until all ingredients are well blended. Combine blueberries with the flour and gently fold into batter. Fill 18 paper-lined muffins cups 3/4 full. Bake in preheated 350° oven for 40 minutes.

Copper Miners' Bread

1/2 cup MILK	2 cups FLOUR
1/2 cup WATER	1/2 tsp. SALT
1 EGG	1 Tbsp. BAKING POWDER
4 Tbsp. BACON DRIPPINGS	

In a small bowl, combine milk, water, egg and bacon drippings. In a large bowl, combine the flour, salt and baking powder. Gradually stir in the milk mixture. Pour dough into a greased loaf pan and bake for 40 minutes in a 350° oven.

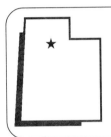

Bingham Canyon Copper

Daniel C. Jackling made the open pit mining of low-grade ore profitable at his mines near Bingham Canyon. A fortune in copper was taken from those mines early in the twentieth century.

Cornbread Delight

1 can (15.25 oz.) CREAM-STYLE CORN
1 cup YELLOW CORNMEAL
1 EGG
1/2 tsp. BAKING SODA
1/3 cup melted BUTTER
1 cup CONDENSED MILK
1/2 cup grated CHEDDAR CHEESE
1 can (4 oz.) diced GREEN CHILES

Mix together corn, cornmeal, egg, baking soda, butter and milk until well combined. Spread half of mixture in greased baking pan. Sprinkle a portion of the cheddar cheese on top. Pour the balance of the batter over the cheese. Arrange chiles on top of batter. Sprinkle remaining cheese over mixture. Bake at 350° for approximately 40 minutes or until tests done.

Orange-Cranberry Bread

2 ORANGES	1/2 tsp. BAKING SODA
1 1/2 cup chopped CRANBERRIES	1/2 tsp. SALT
1 cup SUGAR	2 Tbsp. SALAD OIL
2 cups all-purpose FLOUR	1 EGG
1 1/2 tsp. BAKING POWDER	1 cup chopped WALNUTS

Preheat oven to 350°. Squeeze 3/4 cup orange juice and grate 1 1/2 tablespoons orange peel from oranges; set aside. Combine cranberries and 1/4 cup sugar; set aside. In a large bowl mix flour, 3/4 cup sugar, baking powder, baking soda and salt. In a medium bowl, beat oil, egg and orange juice until blended. Stir into flour mixture. Stir in cranberry mixture, walnuts and orange peel. Spoon batter evenly into a greased loaf pan. Bake in a 350° oven for 70 minutes or until a toothpick inserted into center of bread comes out clean. Cool bread in pan for 10 minutes before removing.

Lehi

The sugar beet industry began in Utah in the 1850's when the Mormons first planted beet seeds. The Lehi plant, opened in 1890, was the third in the country to succeed in beet sugar manufacture.

Pioneer Oatmeal Bread

2 cups boiling WATER	1 tsp. SALT
1 cup crushed OATS	4 1/2 cups FLOUR
1 Tbsp. COOKING OIL	2/3 cake compressed YEAST
1/2 cup BROWN SUGAR	1/2 cup lukewarm WATER

Pour boiling water over oats, add cooking oil and soak mixture for 2 hours. Add brown sugar, salt and flour to mixture. Dissolve yeast in lukewarm water and add to oat mixture. Beat well and allow dough to stand until rises and is light. Stir down and shape dough into two loaves. Place in greased loaf pans; let rise until doubled in bulk (about 2 hours) and bake in a 375° oven for 1 hour.

Mormon Muffins

In 1976, when the King family opened the Greenery as part of Rainbow Gardens, they remembered the bran muffins made by their great-grandmother, Nana Chaffin. But, none of them had the recipe. So, the family asked gourmet cooking instructor T. Upton Ramsey of Salt Lake City for help. The following recipe is his interpretation of their childhood memories and is named in dedication to their ancestry.

Robert Peery King—Rainbow Gardens, Ogden

2 cups BOILING WATER
5 tsp. BAKING SODA
1 cup SHORTENING
2 cups SUGAR
4 EGGS
1 qt. BUTTERMILK

5 cups FLOUR
1 tsp. SALT
4 cups ALL BRAN® CEREAL
2 cups 40% BRAN FLAKES®
1 cup chopped WALNUTS

Add baking soda to boiling water and set aside. Whip shortening and sugar until light and fluffy. Add the eggs slowly. Mix well. Add buttermilk, flour and salt and mix well. Add soda water very slowly. Gently fold the cereals and the walnuts into the mix. Let muffin mix sit in the refrigerator over night. Spoon 1/8 cup of mixture into greased muffin tins. Bake at 350° for 30 minutes. Let cool for five minutes.

Makes 3 dozen muffins.

Wasatch Mountain Range

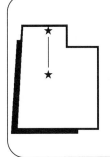

The Wasatch Range extends from Mount Nebo, near Nephi, northward into Idaho. The western side of this rugged range is very steep, rising 6,000 to 8,000 feet above the valleys that border it. The Wasatch Range has many canyons that provide water and serve as recreation areas.

Utah Valley Applesauce Bread

"Applesauce bread can be made a month in advance and frozen for holiday giving. It stays very moist because of the applesauce and slices easily."

Always in Season—Junior League of Salt Lake City, Inc.,
Salt Lake City

4 cups FLOUR	1/2 tsp. NUTMEG
2 Tbsp. CORNSTARCH	1/2 tsp. SALT
2 cups SUGAR	1 cup VEGETABLE OIL
4 tsp. BAKING SODA	3 cups APPLESAUCE
1 tsp. CINNAMON	1 cup RAISINS
1/2 tsp. CLOVES	1/2 cup chopped PECANS
1/2 tsp. ALLSPICE	

Mix the first nine (dry) ingredients in a bowl. In another bowl, combine the rest of the ingredients. Combine both mixtures and mix well. Spoon batter into 2 greased 5 x 9 loaf pans. Bake at 350° for 1 hour. Cool in pans for several minutes; remove to wire racks to cool completely.

Did You Know?

Salt Lake City is known as the "Crossroads of the West" due to its easy access by highway, rail and air.

Banana-Nut Bread

"This recipe was passed down from my great-grandmother."
Penni Hottinger—Tooele Senior Citizens Center, Tooele

1 EGG, beaten	pinch of SALT
1 cup SUGAR	1 tsp. BAKING SODA
1/2 cup OIL	1 cup chopped WALNUTS
3-4 sm. BANANAS	1 cup FLOUR

Combine egg, sugar, oil and bananas. Blend in the balance of ingredients. Pour mixture into a loaf pan and bake for 1 1/2 hours at 350°.

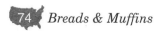

Sourdough Starter

In pioneer days sourdough starter was made by combining flour, salt, sugar, vinegar and water and placing the mixture in a container near a fire to keep it warm. When it began to ferment and bubble, it was set aside to turn sour. This starter dough was used to make breads, pancakes, and biscuits. Each time the starter was used, a cup was held back. More flour and water were added, to replenish the mixture. The original starter mixture was kept for many years.

We have modernized the recipe by using yeast.

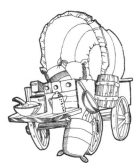

Mormon Sourdough Starter

2 cups WARM WATER
1 pkg. active dry YEAST
2 FLOUR

Place 1/2 cup of warm water in a glass or ceramic bowl, add yeast and allow to dissolve. Add flour and remaining water to mixture. Mix well. Loosely cover mixture and place in a warm place for 3 to 5 days stirring several times a day.

To keep starter active: once a week, add:

1 cup FLOUR
1 cup WARM WATER

Let mixture stand at room temperature either all night or all day before storing in refrigerator.

Sourdough Bread

1 cup SOURDOUGH STARTER (see previous page)
1 quart LUKEWARM WATER
3/4 cup SUGAR
2 Tbsp. SALT
1 cup VEGETABLE OIL
12 cups FLOUR

Add water to sourdough starter followed by the sugar, salt, and oil. Combine just enough flour to dough to make it pliable. Knead dough on lightly floured board until smooth and pliable. Place dough in a greased bowl and allow to rise to twice its size. When ready, punch and knead dough down and again allow it to rise. Divide dough into four sections and place in greased loaf pans. Allow to rise. Bake in 400° oven for 35 to 40 minutes.

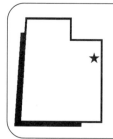

Dinosaur National Monument

One of the world's largest concentrations of fossilized dinosaurs and other prehistoric creatures can be found here. The visitor center near Jensen has over 1,600 fossilized bones and related exhibits.

Sourdough Cornbread

Cornmeal adds its own special rich texture to this recipe.

1 cup SOURDOUGH STARTER
   (see previous page)
1 1/2 cups YELLOW CORNMEAL
1 1/2 cups EVAPORATED MILK
2 EGGS, beaten

2 Tbsp. SUGAR
1/4 cup BUTTER, melted
1/2 tsp. SALT
3/4 tsp. BAKING SODA

Mix the sourdough starter, cornmeal, milk, eggs and sugar thoroughly in a large bowl. Stir in butter, salt and baking soda. Turn into a 10-inch loaf pan and bake at 450° for 30 minutes. Cool on rack before removing from pan.

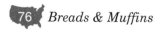

Sourdough Wheat Muffins

1/2 cup WHOLE WHEAT FLOUR
1 1/2 cups ALL-PURPOSE FLOUR
1/2 cup SUGAR
1 tsp. SALT
1 tsp. BAKING SODA

1/2 cup SOURDOUGH STARTER (see page 75)
2 EGGS
1/2 cup SAFFLOWER OIL
1/2 cup EVAPORATED MILK
1 cup RAISINS

Combine all dry ingredients with sourdough starter and mix well. Combine eggs, oil, milk and raisins thoroughly. Fold egg mixture into flour mixture and stir only enough to blend well. Bake in greased muffin pans at 425° for 25 minutes.

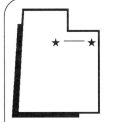

The Uinta Range

The Uinta Range is a part of the Rocky Mountains that extends westward from Colorado almost to Salt Lake City. It is the only major range of the Rocky Mountains that runs east and west. Several peaks in the Uinta Range are more than 13,000 feet high. Kings Peak, the highest point in Utah, rises 13,528 feet near the center of the range.

Sourdough Biscuits

1 1/2 cups FLOUR
2 tsp. BAKING POWDER
1/4 tsp. BAKING SODA
1/2 tsp. SALT

1/4 cup melted BUTTER
1 cup SOURDOUGH STARTER (see page 75)

Sift dry ingredients together. Blend in butter and starter. Pat dough out on a floured surface, adding more flour if needed. Cut into rounds or squares and place on greased baking sheets. Cover and let rise 30 minutes. Bake in a 425° oven for 20 minutes or until brown.

Makes 12 biscuits.

Parmesan-Herb Rolls

This recipe, created by Ruth Kendrick, was a winning entry at the American West Festival Dutch Oven Cookoff which is held the first week of August each year.

American West Heritage Center, Wellsville

1 1/2 cups WARM WATER	1 tsp. dried ROSEMARY
1/2 cup dried MILK	1 tsp. dried THYME
1/3 cup SUGAR	3 Tbsp. PARSLEY
1 Tbsp. YEAST	1/3 cup VEGETABLE OIL
1 EGG, beaten	1 tsp. SALT
2 1/2 cups FLOUR	2 Tbsp. WHIPPING CREAM
3 Tbsp. dried ONION	1/4 cup PARMESAN CHEESE
1 tsp. dried DILL WEED	

Combine warm water, milk, sugar and yeast and allow to set until mixture bubbles. Add egg, flour, onion, dill, rosemary, thyme and parsley. Blend well and allow to set until batter bubbles again. Add vegetable oil, salt and enough flour to make a soft dough. Knead for 5 minutes. Cover and allow to double in size. Form into 13 balls. Place balls in a greased 12-inch Dutch oven. Allow to rise for 10 minutes and then bake, using 8 coals under the oven and 16 coals on the lid. When lightly browned, brush rolls with whipping cream and sprinkle with Parmesan. Bake about 20 minutes or until golden brown.

Pear Bread

3 EGGS, beaten	1 tsp. BAKING SODA
2 cups SUGAR	1/4 tsp. BAKING POWDER
1 cup VEGETABLE OIL	1 tsp. SALT
2 cups chopped PEARS	3 tsp. CINNAMON
2 tsp. VANILLA	chopped WALNUTS
3 cups sifted FLOUR	

In a large bowl, beat together eggs, sugar, and oil. Fold in pears and vanilla. In a medium bowl, sift flour, baking soda, baking powder, salt, and cinnamon together. Combine with pear mixture, add walnuts and mix well. Pour into two greased loaf pans. Bake in a 325° oven for 60 minutes.

Desserts

Lowfat Heaven Sent Chocolate Cake

"This is a wonderfully delicious cake. It is low in fat and very tempting for any chocaholic."

Miriam Bennion—Provo

15 oz. semi-sweet or dark CHOCOLATE
7 Tbsp. unsalted BUTTER
8 large EGGS, separated
2/3 cup SUGAR
2/3 cup BAKING FLOUR

Topping:
   12 oz. semi-sweet or dark CHOCOLATE
   1 1/3 cups sweet WHIPPING CREAM, whipped

Melt chocolate and butter in a double boiler then set aside. Beat egg yolks until light and fluffy. Add sugar slowly to the egg yolk mixture and beat until light yellow in color. Fold in melted chocolate slowly. Add flour gradually and mix gently. Beat egg whites until stiff and fold half of whites into cake mixture. Add balance of whites. Prepare a cake pan and pour cake mixture into it. Bake at 350° for 35 minutes. For topping: melt chocolate and pour slowly into whipped cream. Spread over cooled cake.

Grandma Donna's Cherry Nut Pudding

"This has been a family favorite for years. We especially like to serve it for Christmas and Thanksgiving dinners"

Jennifer Rasmussen—Ogden

1 cup SUGAR	1 Tbsp. melted BUTTER
1 cup FLOUR	1 tsp. BAKING SODA
1/4 tsp. SALT	1 Tbsp. WATER
1 cup PITTED CHERRIES, drained	1 cup coarsely broken NUTS
1 EGG, beaten	

Mix together sugar, flour and salt. Add juice drained from cherries and egg; mix well. Combine butter, baking soda and water. Add to cake batter. Fold in cherries and nuts. Bake in a buttered, 1 1/2 quart casserole at 425° for 30 minutes or until set. Remove from oven and pour **Brown Sugar Sauce** over top while still hot. Allow to stand until cool.

Brown Sugar Sauce

1 Tbsp. BUTTER	1 cup BROWN SUGAR
1 Tbsp. FLOUR	1 tsp. SALT
1 cup HOT WATER	1 tsp. VANILLA

In a saucepan, melt butter; blend in flour. Add hot water and stir until blended. Add brown sugar, salt and vanilla and bring to a boil, stirring constantly.

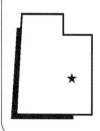

Castle Dale

The area known as the San Rafael Swell, just south of Castle Dale, was the site of Robbers Roost, the hideout of Butch Cassidy and many other outlaws who ranged throughout the state rustling cattle and holding up unwary residents and travelers.

Lime Divine

"A mainstay at Utah reunions and receptions, Lime Divine has become a cultural culinary representation of family fun! It has also inspired the official Green Jell-O Olympic Pin."

Robert Peery King—Rainbow Gardens, Ogden

1 can (16 oz.) PEAR HALVES, undrained
5-8 sprigs FRESH MINT
1 pkg (6 oz.) LIME JELL-O®
1 1/2 cups carbonated LEMON-LIME BEVERAGE
2 Tbsp. LEMON JUICE
1 pkg. (8 oz.) CREAM CHEESE, softened
1/4 cup chopped PECANS

Drain pears, reserving liquid. Dice pears; set aside. Add water to reserved pear liquid to make 1 1/2 cups; place in a saucepan, add mint sprigs and bring to a boil. Put gelatin in a bowl and add boiling liquid; allow to dissolve fully. Remove mint sprigs, add carbonated beverage and lemon juice and combine. Pour 3/4 cup gelatin into a 5-cup mold. Refrigerate for one half hour, until thickened. Arrange 1/2 cup of diced pears in thickened gelatin in the mold. In a large bowl, whisk the balance of the gelatin gradually into cream cheese until smooth. Refrigerate for one half hour or until thickened slightly. Stir in remaining pears, add pecans and spoon mixture over gelatin layer in the mold. Refrigerate 4 hours or until firm. Release from mold and garnish as desired.

Serves 10.

Park City

Millions of dollars of silver were mined from this area, but more recently tourists and skiers have been the mainstay of this city's economy. Park City is home to the U. S. Ski Team and Ski Association. The Sundance Film Festival in January premiers the works of independent filmmakers.

Honey Taffy

"This recipe came from my grandmother's mother."

Bonnie Kelsey—Bountiful

1 1/2 cups HONEY
2 Tbsp. BUTTER, divided
1 tsp. VANILLA

In a saucepan, combine honey and one tablespoon butter; boil until a test drop crackles in cold water. Add the second tablespoon of butter and the vanilla; stir. Cool enough to handle and then pull the candy until it is a light golden color, gets hard and starts to set. Cut with scissors to the desired length.

Did You Know?

St. George's mid-October weather and altitude are perfect for The Huntsman World Senior Games (for athletes 50 and older). The games draw participants from all over the world. The event sponsors worldwide peace, friendship and health.

Pumpkin Custard

Priscilla Lunn—Salt Lake City

3 1/2 cups SKIM MILK
1 tsp. VANILLA
2 EGGS, beaten

1 can (16 oz.) PUMPKIN
3 pkgs. SUGAR SUBSTITUTE
1 tsp. ALLSPICE

Heat milk to hot, not scalding. Add vanilla to milk; set aside. In a bowl, mix together eggs, pumpkin, sugar substitute and allspice. Add hot milk slowly to pumpkin mixture. Pour into a baking pan. Add hot water to a large pan and set baking pan in it. Bake in preheated 350° oven for approximately one hour or until tests done.

Potica Nut Roll

(Po-teet-sa)

"My grandparents came to America from Yugoslavia in 1900. Their country was renamed Slovenia in 1992. The Slovenian Days events are hosted by the Slovene National Benefit Society #757 to celebrate our heritage."

Joanne Lessar—Price

2 cakes DRY YEAST	1/3 cup SUGAR
1/2 cup WARM MILK	1/4 cup BUTTER
1 Tbsp. SUGAR	3 EGGS, well beaten
6 cups sifted FLOUR	1 cup WARM SOUR CREAM
2 tsp. SALT	

Dissolve yeast in the warm milk. Add the sugar to the yeast and set aside. In a separate bowl, mix the remaining ingredients in order given and then add to the yeast mixture. If dough seems to be too dry, add a little more milk (1/4 cup). Mix dough well and knead it at least 10 minutes. Divide dough into 6 balls. Grease each ball lightly and set them in a covered bowl. Let rise in a warm place for 30 to 60 minutes.

On a lightly floured surface, roll out each ball of dough to a 13 x 13-inches (about 1/8-inch thick). Brush surface of dough with melted butter. Spread a sixth of the ***Potica Nut Filling*** (see next page) on the surface of each layer of dough, leaving a space (1/4-inch) on three sides and 4-5-inches on the last side (the top) free of filling. Fold all edges over (makes a better crust). Starting at the bottom, roll up dough jelly-roll style. Prick each roll with a tooth pick on all sides, tops and bottoms about every inch or so. Spread beaten egg over surface of all of the rolls. Place in greased loaf pans and cover with a cloth. Let stand in a warm place for one hour. Bake for 30 minutes at 350° and then lower heat to 325° and bake for another 30 minutes. When done, let cool for 5-10 minutes then remove from pans and brush with melted butter. Wrap immediately in plastic wrap while still warm.

(Continued on next page)

(***Potica Nut Roll*** continued from previous page)

Potica Nut Filling

2 lbs. ground WALNUTS
8 oz. WHIPPING CREAM
SUGAR and HONEY to taste
1 stick BUTTER, melted
2 Tbsp. VANILLA

1 tsp. grated LEMON RIND
1 tsp. grated ORANGE RIND
1 tsp. BRANDY
1 tsp. RUM

Combine all ingredients and refrigerate.

Fruita Fritters

1/3 cup SUGAR
1/2 cup MILK
1 EGG
2 Tbsp. VEGETABLE OIL
2 cups FLOUR

2 1/2 tsp. BAKING POWDER
1/2 tsp. SALT
1 can (15 oz.) CLING PEACHES,
    drained and diced
OIL for frying

Mix together sugar, milk, egg and oil. In another bowl, combine flour, baking powder and salt. Add flour mixture to liquid mixture. Stir lightly. Add peaches (or other fruit). Drop by teaspoon into oil heated to 365°. Deep-fry until uniformly brown. Drain on paper. Ice with ***Butter Glaze Icing*** by dipping fritters in icing and draining on a rack.

Butter Glaze Icing

2/3 cup POWDERED SUGAR
1/3 cup MILK

3 Tbsp. BUTTER
1/2 tsp. VANILLA

Combine sugar, milk and butter in saucepan. Cook and stir until boiling. Remove from heat. Add vanilla. Let glaze set for 5 minutes before glazing fritters.

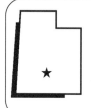

Mormon pioneers established a settlement called Fruita within present-day Capitol Reef National Park. The peach, pear, crab apple and apricot trees that they planted along the Fremont river can still be found here though little remains of the settlement.

Garden City Raspberry Squares

"Our Raspberry Festival (the first full weekend in August), features our local delicacy in a variety of wonderful baked goods, as well as raspberry popsicles and shakes."

Garden City Raspberry Festival Committee—Garden City

1 pkg. VANILLA WAFERS, crushed fine
1/2 cup BUTTER
1 cup POWDERED SUGAR
2 EGGS, separated and beaten
1/2 cup chopped ALMONDS
1 pt. RASPBERRIES
1/2 cup SUGAR
1/2 pt. WHIPPING CREAM

Put half of crushed wafers in 9 x 9 cake pan. Cream butter and powdered sugar, add beaten egg yolks. Fold in stiffly beaten egg whites. Spread over crumbs in pan. Sprinkle with most of the almonds. Crush berries lightly and mix with 1/2 cup sugar; layer over almonds. Top all with whipping cream. Sprinkle remaining nuts and crushed wafers over top of cream. Cover with waxed paper and set in refrigerator to chill for 12 hours or more. Serve with topping of whipped cream and cherries for garnish. Cut in squares.

Serves 10-12.

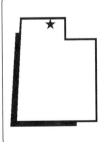

Garden City

Garden City, on the shores of famous Bear Lake, is host to thousands of visitors each year that come to enjoy the white sandy beaches and crystal clear water of this 160-square-mile lake. Four state parks on the shores of this beautiful lake offer all that recreationalists could desire.

Mayonnaise Cake

"This is a very moist cake that my mother used to make when she didn't have eggs on hand."

Linda Deyo—Tooele Senior Center, Tooele

2 cups FLOUR	1/2 cup WATER
1/2 Tbsp. BAKING SODA	4 Tbsp. powdered COCOA
1 Tbsp. BAKING POWDER	1 cup MAYONNAISE
1 cup SUGAR	

Combine flour, baking soda and baking powder together in a large bowl. In another bowl, combine sugar, water, cocoa and mayonnaise. Combine both ingredients and pour into cake pan. Bake for 30-35 minutes at 350°. Test for doneness with a toothpick. When it comes out clean from the center of cake, remove from oven.

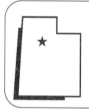

Tooele

Ezra Taft Benson built a grist mill here in 1854 to serve the early Mormon settlers. The site also includes a pioneer cabin, a 1920 blacksmith shop and the miller's home.

Red Devil's Food Cake

"My mother, Eva Twitchell, brought this recipe to Utah in 1914 as a young bride."

Bea Gleave—Senior Center, Monroe

2 cups SUGAR	2/3 cup COCOA
1/2 cup BUTTER	1/2 cup BOILING WATER
2 EGGS, well beaten	1 tsp. VANILLA
1/2 cup SOUR MILK	1/4 tsp. SALT
1 heaping tsp. BAKING SODA	2 1/2 cups sifted FLOUR

Cream butter and sugar together. Stir in eggs and sour milk. Dissolve baking soda and cocoa in boiling water and add to the butter mixture. Stir in vanilla and salt and blend in flour. Pour into cake pans and bake for 35-40 minutes in a 350° oven.

Peach Dessert Cake

"This was a winning recipe in one of our past Peach Days Bake Offs (held the second weekend every September)."

Peach Days Celebration—Brigham City

1 cup **CAKE FLOUR**
1 tsp. **BAKING POWDER**
1/4 tsp. **SALT**
1/2 cup **SUGAR**
1/2 cup **SHORTENING**
1 tsp. grated **LEMON RIND**
2 **EGGS**, unbeaten
4 **RIPE PEACHES**, peeled and sliced
1/3 cup **SUGAR**
1/2 tsp. **CINNAMON**
1/4 cup chopped **WALNUTS or PECANS**

Sift flour, baking powder and salt together. Beat 1/2 cup sugar and shortening until light. Add lemon rind, then eggs, one at a time; beating well. Add flour mixture in fourths, beating after each addition. Spread half of the batter in a greased 8 x 8 baking pan. Top with peaches. Combine 1/3 cup sugar, cinnamon and nuts; sprinkle over all. Bake 50 minutes at 350°. Cut into squares and top with whipped cream.

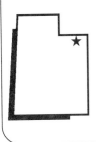

Flaming Gorge

Lake Flaming Gorge, created by the Flaming Gorge Dam at Dutch John, is 91-miles-long. The National Recreation Area, which crosses the border between Utah and Wyoming consists of the lake and Flaming Gorge and Red canyons. A complete 160-mile loop can be driven around the recreation area.

Chocolate Lovers' Favorite Mint Brownies

A Pinch of Salt Lake—Junior League of Salt Lake City, Inc.,
Salt Lake City

2 cups SUGAR	2 1/2 cups sifted FLOUR
1 cup BUTTER, softened	1/4 tsp. SALT
4 EGGS	1/4 tsp. BAKING POWDER
4 (1-oz.) squares unsweetened	2 tsp. VANILLA EXTRACT
CHOCOLATE, melted and	1 cup broken WALNUTS or
slightly cooled	PECANS

Preheat oven to 325°. In a large bowl, cream together sugar and butter until fluffy. Beat in eggs until well blended; then add melted chocolate. Sift flour, measure, sift again with dry ingredients and add to creamed mixture along with vanilla and nuts. Spread in a greased and floured 9 x 13 baking pan and bake for 30 to 35 minutes or until no imprint is left when top is touched with finger. Spread **Mint Frosting** over top and refrigerate for one hour. Glaze with **Chocolate Chip Glaze Topping.**

Mint Frosting

4 Tbsp. BUTTER, softened	1/2 tsp. PEPPERMINT EXTRACT
2 Tbsp. EVAPORATED MILK	Few drops RED or GREEN
2 cups POWDERED SUGAR	FOOD COLORING

Mix all frosting ingredients together until creamy.

Chocolate Chip Glaze Topping

6 Tbsp. BUTTER	2 tsp. VANILLA EXTRACT
1 cup semi-sweet	
CHOCOLATE CHIPS	

In the top of a double boiler, combine butter and chocolate chips. Add vanilla and blend thoroughly. Pour gently over pink or green frosting and spread by tipping pan; refrigerate.

Pineapple Surprise Cake

Dolly Daily—St. George

1 stick BUTTER
2 cups SUGAR
2 EGGS
2 cups FLOUR
1 tsp. BAKING SODA

1 tsp. BAKING POWDER
1 can (16 oz.) CRUSHED
    PINEAPPLE, undrained
1 tsp. VANILLA
1/2 cup PECANS

Cream butter, sugar and eggs together. Add flour, baking soda and baking powder and mix well. Stir in pineapple (include juice), vanilla and pecans. Pour mixture into a 9 x 13 cake pan and bake for 45 to 60 minutes at 350°. Cool and frost with *Cream Cheese Frosting*.

Cream Cheese Frosting

1 pkg. (8 oz.) CREAM CHEESE
1 tsp. VANILLA

1 3/4 cups POWDERED SUGAR
1/2 cup chopped PECANS

Combine cream cheese, vanilla and sugar until smooth. Blend in pecans.

Crazy Crust Peach Cobbler

"This recipe was given to me by my daughter-in-law who received it from her grandmother."

Deon Mayberry—Beehive Homes of Ogden, Clearfield & Roy

1 stick BUTTER, melted
1 cup SUGAR
1 cup CANNED MILK
1 cup FLOUR

1 Tbsp. BAKING POWDER
1 tsp. SALT
1 can (16 oz.) sliced PEACHES,
    undrained

Melt butter in a 9 x 13 baking dish. Add sugar and milk and blend with a fork. Add flour, baking powder and salt and mix just until smooth. Pour peaches over top (including juice). Sprinkle with sugar and bake at 350° for 30 minutes or until crust is golden brown. Serve warm with ice cream.

Index

Index (continued)

Index (continued)

Utah Cook Book
Recipe Contributors

American West Heritage Center, Wellsville—Jeff Courier & Dick Hill 35,
    Janet Froh 41, Kent Mayberry & Brian Terry 47, Ruth Kendrick 78
Karen Anderson, Provo 43
Deon Mayberry—Beehive Homes of Ogden, Clearfield & Roy 89
Meriam Bennion, Provo 79
Lamar Cox, Payson 20
Dolly Daily, St. George 82, 89
Iantha Folkman—Brigham City Senior Center, Brigham City 27-28, 46
Jim & Karyn Clark, St. George   13,19, 22
Ruby Dutson, Layton   44
Jerrie Finley, Salt Lake City   43
Chris Freymuller, Salt Lake City   52
Garden City Raspberry Festival, Garden City 85
Chef Todd Gardiner—Iron Blossom Lodge, Wildflower   53
Bea Gleave, Senior Center, Monroe 86
Leah Probst Godfrey, Midway 68
Maria Harnell, Bountiful   49
LaRee P. Hunt, Midway 68
Junior League of Salt Lake City (see page 2) 18, 40, 54, 70, 74, 88
Bonnie Kelsey, Bountiful 82
Athena Kontas, Price   9
Joanne Lessar, Price 83
Chef David Jones—Log Haven Restaurant, Salt Lake City 56
Priscilla Lunn, Salt Lake City 82
National Cattlemen's Beef Association   37
Lynette Nelson, Salt Lake City   42
Joyce Parrish, Salt Lake City 38
Peach Days Celebration, Brigham City 87
Robert Peery King—Rainbow Gardens, Ogden   16, 73, 81
Rachel Rassmussen, Ogden 59
Jennifer Rassmussen, Ogden   80
Nancy Saxton—Saltair Bed & Breakfast, Salt Lake City 16
Donna Curtis—Seven Wives Inn, St. George   17
Aldine Smith, Salt Lake City   23
Pat Conover—Editor, Springville Herald, Springville   29
Lucy Thompson, Midway 68
Chef Mike Henson—350 Main-Seafood & Oyster Company   45
Linda Deyo, Tooele Senior Center, Tooele 86
Penni Hottinger—Tooele Senior Citizens Center, Tooele   74
Utah Cattle Women & Utah Beef Council, Salt Lake City 29, 32, 55
Becky Low—USU Home Economics Ext., Salt Lake City 60, 69
Bonnie Van Ausdal Hall, Santaquin 39
Martha Vance, Provo   65